R. Barry O'Brien

The Parliamentary History of the Irish land Question

From 1829 to 1869: and the Origin and rResults of the Ulster Custom. Fourth

Edition

R. Barry O'Brien

The Parliamentary History of the Irish land Question
From 1829 to 1869: and the Origin and rResults of the Ulster Custom. Fourth Edition

ISBN/EAN: 9783744721240

Printed in Europe, USA, Canada, Australia, Japan

Cover: Foto ©Suzi / pixelio.de

More available books at **www.hansebooks.com**

THE

PARLIAMENTARY HISTORY

OF

THE IRISH LAND QUESTION,

From 1829 *to* 1869;

AND

THE ORIGIN AND RESULTS OF

THE ULSTER CUSTOM.

By R. BARRY O'BRIEN,

OF THE MIDDLE TEMPLE, BARRISTER-AT-LAW; AUTHOR OF "THE IRISH LAND
QUESTION AND ENGLISH PUBLIC OPINION."

FOURTH EDITION.

London :

SAMPSON LOW, MARSTON, SEARLE, & RIVINGTON,

CROWN BUILDINGS, 188, FLEET STREET.

1880.

LONDON :
GILBERT AND RIVINGTON, PRINTERS,
ST. JOHN'S SQUARE.

PREFACE.

IN the following pages I have endeavoured to trace, from authentic sources, the parliamentary history of the Irish Land Question. That question has a history apart from and reaching far beyond the limits prescribed in my text ; but with this more extended area of events I do not deal, contenting myself with a concise narrative of legislative efforts, and facts and circumstances connected with them, from 1829 to 1870. I have throughout preferred to let others speak rather than to speak myself. The names of the men to whose utterances I invite attention are well known wherever the English tongue is spoken. My object has been not to enforce opinions or advance theories of my own, but by this collection and array of evidence to lay before the public materials on which they may, perhaps, be enabled to arrive at sound conclusions on the Irish Land Question.

R. BARRY O'BRIEN.

Temple, Nov. 1, 1880.

PREFACE TO SECOND EDITION.

ALTHOUGH the necessity for issuing rapidly a second edition of this work leaves little time for supplementing what I had originally written, I desire to add something with reference to certain provisions of the Land Act of 1870 but slightly touched upon in the text.

I have therefore briefly stated in a Note, at page 222, such details respecting those provisions as I deemed essential for more fully comprehending the nature and scope of Mr. Gladstone's Act.

R. BARRY O'BRIEN.

Temple, November 25th, 1880.

CONTENTS.

THE PARLIAMENTARY HISTORY OF
THE IRISH LAND QUESTION.

I.

INTRODUCTORY.

ON the passing of the Catholic Relief Bill, in 1829,
a season of repose supervened in Ireland. Mr.
Doherty, the Irish Solicitor-General of the day,
stated in the House of Commons, early in 1830,
that the Catholic priests, who a year before had
been discontented, were now employed in pouring
forth their admonitions of peace and good-will.
"Emancipation," he added, "has done all the good
that had been hoped for, and none of the harm that
was apprehended."[1] O'Connell's first speech upon
the Irish land question in the House of Commons,
delivered on the 16th February, 1830, was a marvel
of moderation and good temper ; a fact as to
the reassuring value of which Lord Althorp made

[1] Hansard (Feb. 16, 1830).

B

special allusion.[2]   Indeed, the attitude assumed
at the time by the Irish people and their leaders
afforded ample proof of the good effects which a
policy of justice and reparation would be sure to
produce in Ireland.   There was, however, a great
deal of distress in the country, and many evils
which could not be touched by the emancipation
of the Catholics remained still in need of prompt
and vigorous treatment.   "Emancipation," as Mr.
Froude has said, "could not drain the bogs, build
houses, plough and plant the soil, teach the owners
of it wisdom, or the peasants who dwelt upon it
industry."[3]

The Land Question remained to be dealt with,
and there were not wanting then, as there are not
wanting now, unmistakable signs that until this
difficult problem was solved, peace and contentment would not prevail for long in Ireland.

I have already, elsewhere, endeavoured briefly
to sketch the history of the Irish land system—
to state how it sprang up ; how it was maintained.[4]
Lord Palmerston once said that the "evils of
Ireland were to be traced to the history of Ireland."[5]   It may with equal truth be stated that

[2] Hansard (Feb. 16, 1830).

[3] "Romanism and the Irish Race," by James A. Froude,
North American Review, Jan. 1880, p. 38.

[4] "The Irish Land Question and English Public Opinion."

[5] Hansard (May 4, 1855).

the evils of the land system are to be traced to the history of the land system. Its history is, in a large degree, the history of Ireland. Without some knowledge of that history the question can never be solved—never be understood. It is not my intention now to revert at any length to the historical phase of the subject, nor to dwell upon the disorders engendered by the system of land tenure in Ireland. It is my present purpose solely to consider what steps have been taken by the Parliament of England to remove those disorders. Nevertheless, I cannot refrain from placing before my readers the following extract, bearing upon the historical aspect of the subject, taken from the pen of Mr. Froude :—

"Of all the fatal gifts," says Mr. Froude, "which we bestowed on our unhappy possession was the English system of owning land. Land, properly speaking, cannot be owned by any man—it belongs to all the human race. Laws have to be made to secure the profits of their industry to those who cultivate it ; but the private pro-perty of this or that person, which he is entitled to deal with as he pleases, land never ought to be, and never strictly is. In Ireland, as in all primitive civilizations, the soil was divided among the tribes. Each tribe collectively owned its own district. Under the feudal system the proprietor was the Crown, as representing the nation; while the subordinate tenures were held with duties attached to them, and were liable on non-fulfil-ment to forfeiture. In England the burden of defence was on the land. Every gentleman, according to his estate, was bound to bring so many men into the field, properly armed and accoutred. When a standing army was substi-tuted for the old levies, the country squires served as unpaid magistrates on the commission of the peace. The country squire system was, in fact, a development of the feudal system, and, as we gave the feudal system to Ireland, so we tried long and earnestly to give them our landowners. The intention, doubtless, was as good as pos-sible in both cases, but we had taken no trouble to understand Ireland, and we failed as completely as before. The duties attached to landed pro-perty died away, or were forgotten—the owner-ship only remained. The people, retaining their tribal traditions, believed that they had rights upon the land on which they lived. The owner believed that there were no rights but his own. In England the rights of landlords have simi-larly survived their duties, but they have been modified by custom or public opinion. In Ire-land, the proprietor was an alien, with the for-tunes of the residents upon his estates in his hands, and at his mercy. He was divided from them in creed and language; he despised them, as of an inferior race, and he acknowledged no interest in common with them. Had he been allowed to trample on them, and make them his slaves, he would have cared for them, perhaps, as he cared for his horses. But their persons were free, while their farms and houses were his; and thus his only object was to wring out of them the last penny which they could pay, leaving them and their children to a life scarcely raised above the level of their own pigs."[6]

The concluding words of this passage describe what the condition of the Irish peasant farmer was previous to, and during a great portion of the period covered by these pages. Addressing the House of Commons on the 11th of November, 1830, the Irish Solicitor, to whom I have already referred,[7] said, that there was then in Ireland the existence of a condition of things which the lower animals in England would scarcely endure, and which, in fact, they did not endure.[8]

Catholic Emancipation, while powerfully affecting his politico-religious status, in no wise benefited the Irish tenant as such; indeed, it may be

[6] "Romanism and the Irish Race," p. 36.
[7] Ante, p. 1.
[8] Hansard (Nov. 11, 1830).

said that, in some respects, its operation brought him serious injury.[9]

To make this clear a brief reference to antecedent history is necessary. In 1793 a Relief Bill had been carried through the Irish Parliament, admitting Catholics to the elective franchise.[1] It thus became advantageous to the landlords to keep their tenants, the vast majority of whom belonged to the ancient faith, on the land, at all events. The tenant was worth preserving, for the sake of his vote, which the landlord always controlled, if for no other reason. So far the tenant had "fixity of tenure." His condition was miserable ; but his position, such as it was, secure. "It is said," observes Mr. Butt, "that the existence of the forty-shilling franchise encouraged, to a very injurious extent, the subdivision of land. Both the extent, and the mischief of creating a number

[9] A Catholic clergyman, examined upon one occasion before a parliamentary committee, was asked what he believed to be the object of the illegal combinations then prevalent amongst the tenant classes. He answered, "to keep themselves on the land. I have often heard their conversations, when they say, ' What good did the emancipation do us ? Are we better clothed or fed, or are our children better clothed or fed ? ' " *Vide* Butt's " Land Tenure in Ireland," p. 109 n.

[1] Lecky's " Leaders of Public Opinion in Ireland," p. 216. The Act of 1793 had given to every person possessed of a forty-shilling freehold the right to vote for members of parliament.

of small tenements for the sake of making free-holders, have been very much exaggerated. But even this, as far as it extended, caused the exist-ence of a number of occupiers holding by a settled tenure. The mischief was not in the lease, or even in the subdivision, but in the causes which re-duced the occupier to the condition of a serf." [2]

The practice of subdivision—whether its mischief has been very much exaggerated or not—was encouraged by landlords and middle-men for poli-tical purposes. "Landlords and middle-men," says the Report of the Devon Commission, "found the importance of a numerous following of tenantry, and subdivision and sub-letting being by this law" (the Act of 1793) "indirectly encouraged, greatly increased." [3] "Landlords," corroborates Mr. Jephson, in his "Notes on Irish Questions," "con-sidering that every freehold they created added so much to their personal and political interest in the country, often, on the expiration of a lease, cut up their farms into several smaller holdings, for the purpose of multiplying voters, and encouraged their leaseholders to divide their lands for the same purpose." [4] Finally, Mr. Lecky says, "The land

[2] "Land Tenure in Ireland," p. 35.
[3] "Digest of Devon Commission," vol. ii. p. 1109.
[4] "Notes on Irish Questions," by Henry L. Jephson, p. 17.

was divided into infinitesimal farms. Many landlords, bound by their leases, were unable to interfere with the process of division, while others
acquiesced in it through laxity of temper or
dread of unpopularity, and others encouraged it,
as the multiplication of forty-shilling freeholders
increased the number of voters whom they could
control."[5] So far the tenants were allowed, and
much encouraged to fasten themselves upon the
land. But the importation into the Catholic
Emancipation Act of a clause by which the forty-
shilling freeholders were disfranchised, changed all
this. The peasant tenant was no longer a political
factor. The landlord's interest in his political
existence was, so far, diminished. If, in other
respects, it suited the landlord's purpose to remove
him, no countervailing motives now prevailed to
restrain his action. So it was that the clearance
system became a result of Catholic Emancipation.
I do not mean to allege that there were no
"clearances" until after Catholic Emancipation.
Clearances there were after the Sub-letting Act
of 1826,[6] and even at a time previous to that date.

[5] Lecky's "Leaders of Public Opinion in Ireland," p. 255.

[6] This Act (7 Geo. IV. c. 28) prohibited the sub-letting of
property by a lessee, unless with the express consent of the
proprietor. *Vide* Jephson's "Notes on Irish Question," p. 57.
The following extract upon this subject from Mr. McCullagh
Torrens' "Life of Lord Melbourne" may be worth quoting

"It is a mistake to imagine," says the report of a Select Committee of the House of Commons in 1830, "that clearances of estates have originated with the Sub-letting Act, or with the statute that raised the franchise. On the contrary, they existed more than ten years before those measures were adopted; but it is undoubtedly true that both statutes have given motives, or afforded facilities for pursuing a course previously adopted on the ground of personal interest." [7]   In fine, it was not until the petty tenants ceased to be of political weight, that the system of clearances and consolidation grew into formidable dimensions in Ireland.

here: "One of the last measures of importance carried by the Liverpool Administration was the Sub-letting Act, applicable only to Ireland. For many years a constant theme of censure by economic writers and reports of select committees had been the excessive partition of the soil for the purpose of creating forty-shilling freeholds. Crowds of sub-tenants were yearly multiplied—not only impoverished by usurious exaction, but were subjected to the risk, and often to the loss, of what little they possessed by process of distraint for default in payment of rent by the middle-man under whom they held. Nothing but a disabling law would, it was supposed, check this fertile source of disquietude and misery; and in 1826 an enactment was passed rendering null and void sub-leases or sub-assignments of land without regard to the depreciation of the interests for which fines had frequently been given by the primary lessees." (McCullagh Torrens' "Life of Lord Melbourne," vol. i. p. 311.)

[7] "Report of Select Committee House of Commons, 1830," p. 8.

II.

1596 TO 1829.

THE great distress which prevailed throughout Ireland in 1829 attracted the attention of the Government. Mr. Brownlow, a landlord and an Ulster member, stated in the House of Commons, on the 26th February, 1829, that the condition of the people was beyond description, adding that "in no part of the world was such complicated suffering borne with such exemplary patience." All the public records of the day contain abundance of evidence in corroboration of Mr. Brownlow's statement. Indeed, the subject of Irish distress was even then not an unfamiliar one to the Parliament of England. Many years later Mr. Roebuck, alluding to the representations so frequently made, and to the demands for Government assistance so often urged by the Irish members, spoke of their utterances as the "moan of beggars" and the "whine of mendicants."[1] Upon another

[1] Hansard (Feb. 27, 1865).

occasion Mr. Bright declared that the "pivot on
which the Government of Ireland had turned had
been force and alms."[2]   Too true.   This is the
history of Ireland since the Union summed up in
a single sentence.   A history of Coercion Bills, of
charitable doles meted out at painfully recurring
intervals—always given freely and generously by
the people of England, but not always extracted
without difficulty from the Government of England—and of select committees, whose inquiries
and reports produced no practical results.   Sir
Robert Peel stated, in 1829, that in scarcely one
year since the Union was Ireland governed by
ordinary law.[3]   The Habeas Corpus Act had been
suspended in the country in 1800, from 1802 till
1805, from 1807 till 1810, in 1814, and from 1822
till 1824.[4]   There were select committees upon
Ireland almost every year since the Union.[5]
Whenever disturbances arose, and distress appeared, Coercion Acts were passed, and select
committees appointed.

Nothing more was done.   A goodly volume
might be filled with forcibly apposite extracts

[2] " Annual Register," 1849, p. 72.
[3] Doubleday's " Life of Sir R. Peel," vol. i. pp. 482, 483.
[4] Lecky's " Leaders of Public Opinion in Ireland,"
p. 261.
[5] " Index to Parliamentary Papers from 1801 to 1829."

from the proceedings of the numerous select committees appointed to inquire into the condition of
Ireland since the Union. The reports of all these
committees, and the minutes of evidence given
before them, might be perused with profit by
those who desire to bring about a satisfactory
and final solution of the Irish land question. I
have sometimes heard the opinion expressed that
the history of that question only commenced
with the Devon Commission in 1845. This opinion
is an erroneous one. The history of the Irish land
question is of much older date. In truth, it is as
old as the conquest of Ireland by England. It
grew out of that conquest, and has existed ever
since ; because, unhappily, the policy of conquest
has been perpetuated from generation to generation. The incidents of Irish landlordism are
the natural outcome of a system founded on conquest and confiscation. They have sprung up as
the inevitable results of the act which forced an
alien and conqueror-proprietary on a defeated
people ; and they have been preserved down to our
own times, because the descendants of the original
grantors on the one hand, and of the native population on the other, have retained the prejudices
and the antipathies of their respective ancestors.
The distinguishing features of Irish landlordism
remain the same in many respects in the days of

Victoria as they were in the days of Elizabeth. Uncertainty of tenure was the evil then. It is in the main the evil now. The Anglo-Irish landlord was an absentee then. He is in the main an absentee to-day.[6]

Spenser, writing in 1596 with reference to the relation of landlord and tenant in Ireland at that time, says, " Now we will proceede to other like defects, amongst which there is one generall inconvenience, which raigneth almost throughout all Ireland ; that is, the Lords of land and freeholders doe not there use to set out their land in farme, or for tearme of years, to their tennants, but onely from yeare to yeare, and some during pleasure, neither indeede will the Irish tennant or husbandman otherwise take his land, then so long as he list himselfe. The reason hereof in the tennant is, for that the landlords there use most shamefully

---

[6] " In Ireland," said Mr. Bright, speaking in the House of Commons on the 27th of August last, " one-half of the proprietors are supposed to be absentees. I remember talking to a magistrate in one of the centre towns in Ireland, and he said, ' The difficulty is we have no men to put on the bench. If a man has a few thousands a year he resides in London or Paris ; if he has 1000*l.* a year he lives in Dublin ; and looking all round this district in which I act, it is a great misfortune that there are no gentlemen living in the neighbourhood who would be thought suitable by the tenantry to place on the magisterial bench.' "—*Daily Telegraph*, August 27, 1880.

to racke their tennants, exacting of them what
he pleaseth. So that the poore husbandman
either dare not binde himselfe to him for longer
tearme, or thinketh, by his continuall liberty of
change, to keepe his landlord the rather in awe
from wronging of him."

"The 'tennant,'" continues Spenser, "hath no such
state in any his houlding, no such building upon
any farme, no such coste imployed in fensing or
husbanding the same, as might with-hold him from
any such willfull course, as his lord's cause, or his
owne lewde disposition may carry him unto. All
which he hath forborne, and spared so much ex-
pence, for that he had no firme estate in his tenement, but was only a tennant at will or little more,
and so at will may leave it. And this inconvenience may be reason enough to ground any ordi-
nance for the good of the commonwealth, against
the private behoofe or will of any landlord, that
shall refuse to graunt any such terme or estate unto
his tennant, as may tende to the good of the whole
realme.

"Indeede it is a great willfullness in any landlord
to refuse to make any longer farmes unto their
tennants, as may, besides the generall good of the
realme, be also greatly for their own profit and
avail: For what reasonable man will not thinke
that the tenement shall be made much better for

the lord's behoofe, if the tennant may by such good meanes be drawne to build himselfe some handsome habitation thereon, to ditch and enclose his ground, to manure and husband it as good farmers use ? for when his tennants terme shall be expired, it will yield him, in the renewing his lease, both a good fine, and also a better rent. And also it shall be for the good of the tennant likewise, who by such buildings and inclosures shall receive many benefits : first, by the handsomenesse of his house, he shall take more comfort of his life, more safe dwelling, and a delight to keepe his said house neate and cleanely, which now being, as they commonly are, rather swyne-stys than houses, is the chiefest cause of his so beastly manner of life, and savage condition, lying and living together with his beast in one house, in one room, in one bed, that is, clean strawe, or rather a foule dunghill. And to all these other commodities he shall in short time find a greater added, that is his own wealth and riches increased, and wonderfully inlarged, by keeping his cattle in inclosures where they shall alwayes have fresh pasture, that now is all trampled and over-runne ; warme covert, that now lyeth open to all weather ; safe being, that now are continually filched and stolen."[1]

[1] Spenser's " View of the State of Ireland." (" Collected Tracts and Treatises on Ireland," voL i. pp. 504—506.)

Writing two centuries later, and dealing with the same subject, Arthur Dobbs says, "The discouragement to improvements arising from our present method of letting our lands by short leases of twenty-one years, is obvious to all." Places where the numbers of papists are great, it is plain, will never be improved ; on the contrary, they will rather endeavour to waste and impoverish the land, though bound up by the strictest ties.

"This is occasioned by the shortness of their leases. We find very little improvement made upon leases of thirty-one or forty-one years. Let us cast our eyes upon church lands throughout the kingdom, and we will not find one place in a hundred where there is any tolerable improvement made upon them. The bishops (who have only their lands for life, which afterwards go to their successors) by their frequent translations, can scarce expect to be so long fixed in any diocese as to leave their lands to any of their family, and for that reason take fines from three to three years, or from seven to seven years; when they cannot by such tenures prevail with their tenants to improve, how can lay-landlords, whose estates descend to their children, expect their tenants should improve upon leases determinable upon thirty-one or forty-one years, or even three lives ? Have not tenants daily instances before them of landlords squandering away their time and money, and living above their fortunes, upon the prospect they have of retrieving their affairs at the expiration of such leases, by raising extraordinary fines, or setting their lands to those who offer most for them? Upon renewal, the improving tenant must pay for the landlord's extravagance, a sum of money equivalent to the improvement he has made, and the utmost value of the land, in case he has been so provident as to have acquired any money, which seldom happens upon such tenures; or he must give a nominal great rent for the future, if he renews his lease, otherwise the next person who offers a trifle more, gets his lands and he is turned adrift, to serve in like manner the next whose lease is expired. Thus where the landlord proves extravagant, he scarcely ever distinguishes between an improving and a non-improving tenant.

*   *   *   *   *

" How, then, can a tenant improve his land when he is convinced that, after all his care and toil his improvements will be overated, and he be obliged to shift for himself? Let us place ourselves in his situation, and see if we should think it reasonable to improve for another, when these improvements would be the very cause of our being removed from the enjoyment of them. I believe we should not. Industry and improvements go very

C

heavily on when we think we are not to have the property in either. What can be expected, then, from covenants to improve and plant, when the person to do it knows he is to have no property in them? There will be no concern or care taken to preserve them, and they will run to ruin as fast as made or planted. What was it induced so many of the commonalty lately to go to America, but high rents, bad seasons, and want of good tenures, or a permanent property in their lands? This kept them poor and low, that they scarce had sufficient credit to procure necessaries to subsist or till their ground. They never had anything in store, all was from hand to mouth, so one or two bad crops broke them. Others found their stock dwindling and decaying visibly, and so removed before all was gone, whilst they had as much left as would pay their passage, and had little more than would carry them to the American shore. This, it may be allowed, was the occasion of the poor farmers going who had their rents lately raised; but it may be objected, that was not the reason why rich farmers went, and those who had several years in beneficial leases yet unexpired, who sold those bargains, and removed with their effects; but it is plain they all went for the same reason; for these last, from daily examples before them, saw the present occupiers dispossessed of their lands at the expiration of their leases, and no preference given to them, so they expected it would soon be their own case; to avoid which, and make the most of the years yet unexpired, they sold, and carried their effects with them, to procure a settlement in a country where they had reason to expect a permanent property."[8] Upon the Absentee question Prior about the same date writes :—

" We are not now at a loss to point out the principal source of all our misfortunes, and the chief cause of all this distress; it appears plainly, from the list of absentees, and the estimate of the quantity of specie they may be reasonably supposed to draw yearly out of the kingdom, that no other country labours under so wasteful a drain of its treasure, as Ireland does at present, by an annual remittance of above 600,000*l.* to our gentlemen abroad, without the least consideration or value returned for the same : this is so great a burthen upon us that I believe there is not in history an instance of any one country paying so large a yearly tribute to another.

* * * * *

" It is melancholy to observe that now we are labouring under great disadvantages in trade, and

[8] Dobb's " Essay upon the Trade of Ireland." (" Collected Tracts and Treatises on Ireland," vol. ii. pp. 470, 472.)

struggling with penury and want, the humour of living and spending abroad still increases among our men of quality and station, and has even infected our ladies, who may be sooner found out at London, Paris, Rome, or any foreign place of expense than at home.

＊   ＊   ＊   ＊   ＊

" It is too much in reason for these gentlemen to expect that we shall patiently bear with the loss of our trade, loss of our money, and additional taxes, for no other reason, but to gratify the vanity of those who have thus wantonly abandoned their country, and riot abroad in its ruin. There is no way left to save us but by obliging them to live at home, or making them pay for living abroad. . . . I wish we could say that these gentlemen, by living abroad, had any way contributed to the interest of Ireland, but I am afraid they have little merit of this kind to plead ; for, except a very few persons who, upon all occasions, have been willing, industrious, and able to serve us (and which we shall ever, with the greatest gratitude, acknowledge), we know of none of our absentees who, upon emergency, wherein the interest of Ireland was concerned, have had spirit or disposition, interest or weight, or even a sufficient knowledge of the affairs of their own country to do it service ; they are generally either strangers to the circumstances and interests of Ireland, or have no power or qualifications to be of use to it. If we inquire into the motives of this conduct of our gentlemen so injurious to their own, and their country's interest, we shall find that a luxurious manner of living, an affectation of imitating the nobility and gentry of other countries in their expenses, together with the largeness of their fortunes, are the principal motives of their spending all their es· tates abroad; which they seldom fail to incumber with great debts, and frequently sell, either to gratify their present vanity, or to pay for past follies.

"It is a melancholy observation, and fit to be remembered, that almost all the estates, which of late years have been sold in Ireland, have belonged to such of our gentlemen as brought themselves under a necessity of selling, to discharge debts contracted abroad. We can justly date the ruin of several great families from the fatal period of their going to live abroad; and we may now prophetically pronounce the like fate of several others who have of late, or shall hereafter, follow the same course of living, that their lands shall pass away to strangers, and their names be no more heard of. The extinction of such families may probably be no hurt to the public, but then the value of their estates spent abroad is certainly loss to the kingdom; an

English prodigal injures none but his own family, since whatever he squanders goes into the pockets of others of the same country ; but an Irish spendthrift, who commonly makes London or Paris the scene of his extravagance, not only deprives his family, but his country also, of the full value of all he consumes. It has been observed (as another ill effect of living abroad), concerning such of our gentlemen of fortune as happen to marry there, that they and their posterity are for the most part lost to this kingdom. It is shocking to an English lady to think of living in such a poor, despised place as Ireland is, and if she has not made it an article of marriage, as it often is the case, she seldom fails some other way to prevail on an easy husband to forsake his country ; and takes care to breed up her children in the same aversion, and from that time forward we hear no more of them, but by their constant drawing all their rents from hence, and racking their poor tenants. Such deserters, and others also, who can be prevailed upon by their Irish ladies to live abroad, prove the worst enemies to Ireland, by laying it under a continual yearly pillage to their vanity and luxury, without contributing the least farthing towards the support of the government.

*   *   *   *   *

" It cannot be supposed that our Irish landlords,

who live abroad and consume no part of the produce or manufacture of their country, pay the least
share of the duties or taxes thereof ; or relieve any
of its poor, whose miseries they never see ; or make
any improvements who never mean to live among
us.

"Nay, their living abroad seems to have so far
alienated their affections from their country, and
hardened their tempers towards it, that they,
above all others, are remarkable for setting their
estates at a rack-rent, so as hardly to allow a
livelihood to their poor tenants, by whom they are
supported.

"There is no country in Europe which produces
and exports so great a quantity of beef, butter,
tallow, hides, and wool, as Ireland does ; and yet
our common people are very poorly clothed, go
bare-legged half the year, and very rarely taste of
that flesh-meat with which we so much abound. We
pinch ourselves in every article of life, and export
more than we can well spare, with no other effect
or advantage than to enable our gentlemen and
ladies to live more luxuriously abroad. And they
are not content to treat us thus, but add insult to
ill-usage. They reproach us with our poverty, at
the same time that they take away our money ;
and can tell us we have no diversions or entertain-
ments in Ireland for them, when they themselves

disable us from having better by withdrawing from us."[9]

Sixty-two years later (1791) the condition of things in Ireland had not improved, as will appear from the following statement addressed to the Irish Parliament by an eminent Protestant Bishop, Dr. Woodward : " The lower class of the people of Ireland," says Dr. Woodward, "are ill accommodated with lodging, raiment, and even food. And their poverty is likely to continue, with but little mitigation from the following amongst other causes —the exorbitant rent extorted from the poorer tenantry, ever loath and afraid to quit their ancient habitations, by the general method of letting farms to the highest bidder without any allowance for tenant-right, the oppression of duty work which drives the cottager arbitrarily from the tillage of the little spot which he holds at so dear a rent . . . It would shock a tender mind to imagine (if imagination could paint) the miseries to which the bulk of the inhabitants of Ireland are continually exposed by the slightest reverse of fortune, by a single bad season, by occasional disease, or even by the gradual decay of nature."[1]

[9] *Vide* Prior's " List of the Absentees of Ireland." (" Collected Tracts and Treatises on Ireland," vol. ii. pp. 247—258.)

[1] Doctor Woodward, as quoted by Mr. Leader, M.P., Hansard, vol. iii. n.s. p. 1232.

These words were spoken in 1791. In 1800 came the Union, and English statesmen hoped, that, with it, everything would be changed in the political, social, and material condition of the country. A new era of prosperity and contentment would, it was said, now dawn upon Ireland. These hopes were sadly doomed to disappointment. Nineteen years after the Union the condition of the Irish people was still one of misery, wretchedness, and discontent. The relation of landlord and tenant remained unchanged ; the poverty and hardships of the people unrelieved.

In 1819 a Select Committee of the Commons was appointed, under the presidency of Sir John Newport, to inquire into the state of disease, and the condition of the labouring poor in Ireland. The report of this Committee opens by stating that the general distress and deficiency of employment "are so notorious as to render the production of any particular evidence to establish the extent and variety of the evil unnecessary." To mitigate this evil, and to give employment, which should have the twofold effect of relieving the existing misery, and permanently improving the condition of the country, the Committee suggest the adoption of measures for facilitating the development of its agricultural resources. " Upon the subject of agricultural improvement," says the Report, " your

Committee (controlled by the permanent principle of avoiding unnecessarily to tamper with so important a branch of industry, and leaving it to its best encouragement, the operation of a free market, nevertheless), think it necessary to point out the extent to which Ireland may be improved, and its power of production of human food vastly extended."

The Committee then direct attention to the means which might be employed to effect this purpose.

" It appears in evidence " continues the Report, "that there are of reclaimable bog in Ireland 2,000,000 of Irish acres of soil suited to the production of grain ; that the evidence given by scientific persons employed under the Bog Commissions, [2] much facilitate the application of private speculation to such improvements, and that in order to give effect to these suggestions a general inclosure and drainage Act on the principle of that for England would be highly important . . . a reference to the reports alluded to will evince the great source of employment which the improvement of the bogs of Ireland would afford to the population. . . . The mountain districts of Ireland, at present comparatively unproductive, are capable of high improvement. They consist of

[2] *Vide* Appendix A.

1,500,000 Irish acres, of which one-half is suitable for agricultural, and the remainder for much improved pasturage for rearing, or dairy purposes, and the entire evidently suitable for planting, much of the worst of it being old forest land."[3] Suggestion for reclaiming the waste lands of Ireland had been made by other select committees. This was, indeed, the remedy, chiefly pointed at in the earlier days of the land question for correcting the evils which prevailed. These suggestions were, unhappily, not acted upon.[4]

The waste lands of England had been reclaimed by individual exertions, or associated companies, aided in their efforts by legislative enactments, which had the effect of removing any impediments such as those indicated in the case of Ireland by the Report of the Bog Commissioners. In Ireland no similar attempts were made. Why ? Because there was no capital in the country, and because legislative enactments to facilitate the work, and to remove the impediments which checked its initiation, or

---

[3] *Vide* " Report of Select Committee (H.C.) upon the condition of the poor in Ireland, 1819," p. 98 ; also Mr. Nimmo's account of the Drainage of England, inserted in the Appendix to the Report. Parliamentary Papers, June 7, 1819 ; reprinted June 19, 1829.

[4] The institution of Commissioners of Sewers as in England was recommended, as also the drainage of the great bogs and marshes, and the making of legal provision for the repayment

progress, could not be obtained.[5] " The want of
capital," says the Report of the Select Committee of
1819, "unnerves all effort for improvement."[6] Why
was there not capital in Ireland to be employed in de-
veloping the agricultural resources of the country ?
I shall answer this question in the words of the
Report of the Select Committee of 1819, premising
in the first place, that the capital would naturally
be expected to come, and ought to have come, either
from the tenants or the landlords.   But it did not
come from the former because " the general practice
of throwing the expense of buildings and repairs
on the tenant, countervailed the accumulation of
profit in the hands of the farmer and the application thereof to beneficial enterprise in agriculture."[7]   On the other hand the capital was not
supplied by the landlords.   The landlords of
Ireland never spent the income derivable from
their Irish estates in improving those estates, or in
endeavouring, generally, to promote the prosperity
of the country.   " In considering," says the Report,
" the causes which discourage industry in Ireland,
it is impossible to overlook the lamentable circum-

of the necessary outlay. *Vide* Report of Select Committee,
1819, as quoted in Nicholl's " Poor Law," p. 88.

   [5] *Vide* Appendix A.

   [6] Report of Select Committee, House of Commons, of
1819, on the condition of the poor in Ireland, p. 96.

   [7] Report of Select Committee, 1819, p. 97.

stance, almost peculiar to the country, the non-residence of a great proportion of the proprietors, and especially of that portion which could most contribute by their rank, their wealth, and their moral influence to operate beneficially on the habits and comforts of the lower classes. The expenditure of income in England resulting therefrom enhances the claim of Ireland to the generous consideration of parliament." [8] Unhappily the time for acknowledging the claims of Ireland to the generous consideration of the English parliament had not yet come. Many years were destined still to pass before those claims should be recognized by that assembly. The Report of the Select Committee of 1819 was allowed—as the reports of previous committees had been allowed—to lie on the table unnoticed. The facts it brought to light were disregarded. Its suggestions were neglected. Its labours, for all practical purposes, were lost.

In 1823 another Select Committee was appointed. Its report tells the same sad tale of misery and want.[9]

The condition of the people is described as "wretched and calamitous to the last degree." We are told that they lived in a state of the utmost

[8] Report of Select Committee of 1819, p. 97.
[9] *Vide* Parliamentary Papers. Report of Select Committee on the condition of the Poor in Ireland in 1823, p. 5.

destitution, without scarcely an article of furniture
in their miserable cabins, using as bed covering " a
little fern and a quantity of straw thrown over it."
All the witnesses examined before the committee
agreed in attributing the existence of this state of
things to the want of employment. The people
were willing to labour but unhappily had nothing
to do. Yet there were millions of acres of waste
land, in the reclamation of which they might have
been employed with profit to themselves and advantage to the country. But no attempt would be
made by government to facilitate or help local
effort in this direction, and government aid was
absolutely necessary for the purpose. Whilst
admitting the danger attending all interference
with industrial pursuits, which prosper best, when
left to their own natural development, the Committee nevertheless point out, that the state
of Ireland constituted an exception to the general
rule, and that the aid of government in support
of local effort was there absolutely necessary.[1]
However, that aid was not given in time, and
never was given in a way calculated permanently to avert impending or remote disasters,
and to teach the Irish people to look with confi-

[1] Report of Select Committee of Commons on the State
of the Irish Poor in 1823 ; also Sir G. Nicholl's "History of
the Irish Poor Laws," p. 95.

dence, and hope, to the English parliament in an hour of emergency.

In 1825 another crisis arose, and another Select Committee was appointed.[1] Before this committee, the peculiar characteristics and incidents which distinguished the relation of landlord and tenant in Ireland, from that relation in England, were well pointed out by an English landlord, who was also the proprietor of estates in Ireland—Sir Frankland Lewis.

"What are the circumstances in the present law between landlord and tenant which appear to you to conduce to the disturbed state of Ireland?" Sir Frankland Lewis was asked.

"I can answer that question," he said, "only as a landlord, and certainly not as a lawyer. It is impossible for any person who knows the relations between landlord and tenant in England not to be struck with the differences in the relation between landlord and tenant in Ireland. I am imperfectly acquainted with the laws or the circumstances which have brought about that effect. Nothing is more striking in Ireland than that a number of burdens which English landlords are willing to take upon themselves, the Irish landlords do not find it necessary to take upon themselves. In the maintenance of a farm in England, all the expen-

---

[1] *Vide* Report of Select Committee, House of Lords, to inquire into the State of Ireland, 1825.

sive part of the capital employed upon a farm is provided by the landlord ; the houses, the gates, the fences, and the drains are all provided by the landlords.   Everybody knows that in Ireland that is not the practice ; at the same time that the landlord obtains as rent in Ireland a much larger proportion of the value of the produce of the land than he obtains in England, and in parts of Ireland it appears to me that the landlord sometimes obtains for rent more than is produced by the land."[1]

The evidence given by Mr. Nimmo before the committee will also be read with interest.   The eminent engineer was asked to state his opinion of the condition of the peasantry of Ireland.   He replied, " I conceive the peasantry of Ireland to be in general in the lowest possible state of existence. Their cabins are in the most miserable condition, and their food potatoes, with water, without even salt.   I have frequently met persons, who begged of me on their knees, to give them some promise of employment, that from the credit of that they might get the means of support."

" To what cause do you attribute this state of things ?" Mr. Nimmo was further asked.   He replied, " It is unquestionable that the great cause

[1] Minutes of Evidence of Select Committee, House of Lords, to inquire into the State of Ireland, 1825, p. 39.

of the miserable condition [of the people] and of the [prevailing] disturbances is the management of land. There is no means of employment, and no certainty that the peasant has of existence for another year but by getting possession of a portion of land, on which he can plant potatoes. The landlord has, in the eyes of the peasant, the right to take from him in a summary way everything he has, if he is unable to execute those covenants into which he has been obliged to enter from the dread of starvation."

" Do you attribute the distressed state of Ireland to the power which resides in the landlord, and to its abuse?" " I conceive that there is no check to that power. It appears to me that, under the cover of law, the landlord may convert that power to any purpose he pleases. The consequence is, that when he wishes he can extract from the peasant every shilling, beyond bare existence, which can be produced by him from the land. The lower order of peasantry can thus never acquire anything like property; and the landlord, at the least reverse of prices, has it in his power to seize, and does seize, his cow, bed, potatoes in ground, and everything he has, and can dispose of the property at any price."[4]

[4] Select Committee House of Lords, 1825. Minutes of Evidence, pp. 165, 179, and Hansard, vol. xxxii. 3rd ser. p. 185.

D

Space will not permit me to quote any further from the proceedings of this select committee, but I heartily commend the perusal of the report and of the minutes of evidence to every one interested in the settlement of the Irish land question. As with all previous select committees on the subject, the labours of this body led to no practical results. No statesmanlike attempt was made to remove the clear and undoubted evils which the unfortunate relation of landlord and tenant in Ireland produced ; no effort was essayed to protect the fruits of the tenant's industry, and to encourage him in his exertions to cultivate and improve the soil. The Irish tenant was left, as it has recently been suggested he should still be left, to the consideration of the landlord ; and it was no doubt hoped then, as it seems to be hoped now, that "public opinion" would influence him in the direction of justice, humanity, and right. But what was the result of leaving the tenant to the "consideration of the landlord," and the landlord to the influence of "public opinion"? This : that in 1829, as in almost every year since the Union, distress prevailed throughout the country, and the misery of the people attracted the attention of Parliament, and shocked the susceptibilities of every honourable and humane Englishman.

III.

1829 TO 1835.

At the commencement of the Session of 1829, Mr. Brownlow brought the condition of the tenant-farmers and labouring classes in Ireland under the notice of the Government. His speech was nothing, more nor less, than a reproduction of much of the matter contained in the reports and evidence of the various select committees to which I have already referred. He dwelt upon the inactivity of former Governments, and now urged that employment should be given to the people, whose condition was "past description and past endurance,"[1] to save them from starvation. "If," said he, "there are millions of unemployed men in Ireland, there are millions of waste land capable of

---

[1] A few months later (on the 16th Feb., 1830), the Irish Solicitor-General stated in the House of Commons that a great part of the tenantry of Ireland were "worse off than the beasts which browsed upon the land," adding that it was "high time" to make an effort to ameliorate their condition. (Hansard, vol. xxii. n.s. p. 541.)

profitable cultivation." To alleviate the existing
distress, and to lay the foundation for future
beneficial exertion, as well as to provide against
the recurrence of future famine calamities, Mr.
Brownlow asked leave to bring in a Bill to facilitate the drainage of bogs and the reclamation of
waste lands.[1] His proposal was, that every person
possessed of a portion of bog or waste land should
be authorized to apply to the Viceroy to appoint
a commission invested with powers to raise money
for the purpose, and to distrain on the lands which
had been drained or reclaimed. This Bill passed
through the Commons, and was, on the motion of
the Marquis of Downshire (opposed by the Earl of
Wicklow), read a second time in the Lords on the
8th June, 1830.[2] It was then referred to a select
committee. On the 1st July, the report of the
select committee was brought up by the Marquis
of Downshire, who said that, although the committee were unanimous with reference to the
importance of the subject, affecting as it did the
prosperity of Ireland, yet, in consequence of the
state of business in the House, there was no chance
of the bill getting through. "The report," he said,
"stated that there were immense tracts of land now
under bog, peat, or morass, the drainage and im-

---

[1] Hansard, vol. xx. n.s. p. 590.
[2] Hansard, vol. xxv. n.s. p. 86.

provement of which would, at no very great expense, yield a quantity of fertile land, which would amply repay the outlay on its drainage." The report, however, was allowed to lie on the table, and there the matter rested.[4] On the 9th of July an Arms Bill, which the Earl of Radnor denounced as "vexatious and oppressive," was, on the motion of the Duke of Wellington, read a second time in the Lords.[5] It had a more fortunate fate than the Waste Lands Bill. Nothing is more melancholy in the history of English legislation for Ireland than the rapidity with which Coercion Acts have been passed, as compared with the apathy and neglect of Parliament in dealing with remedial measures. I once heard Sir Wilfrid Lawson say, *à propos* of the late Zulu war, that the Zulus were a very fine people, and capable of being greatly improved and civilized ; but, he added, "it seems to me that the only efforts which we have taken up to the present to civilize and improve them have been to shoot them." England has left herself open to the charge that, for many years, her chief efforts to improve the Irish people were to imprison or to hang them. " The gallows," says Mr. Bright, "has been the great preserver in Ireland." [6]

[4] Hansard, vol. xxv. n.s. p. 838.

[5] Hansard, vol. xxv. n.s. p. 1116.

[6] *Vide* Mr. Bright's "Collected Addresses," p. 51. This speech was delivered at Rochdale, in 1867.

The very day on which the Arms Bill was read a second time, Earl Stanhope presented a petition from the people of Kent, complaining of the burdens thrown upon them, by reason of the number of Irish poor in their midst. His lordship pointed out, that, while the Chancellor of the Exchequer (Lord Althorp) had been declaring in the House of Commons that Ireland was in a state of great and general prosperity, the country was actually threatened with famine. The distress arose, he said, from the general want of employment; but the Government instead of supplying that want, or even inquiring into the state of Ireland, had been wasting time over the Retford election petition. The Duke of Wellington was, however, apparently unmoved by the appeal, and the facts of Earl Stanhope. The petition which he presented was allowed to lie on the table, and no further notice was taken of it.[7]

Meanwhile the distress in the country continued steadily to spread. On the 13th of July, 1830, Mr. Henry Grattan drew attention to the fact, stating, as had often been stated before, that the main cause of the suffering, and destitution of the people, was the want of employment. He urged the Government to introduce some measure for the reclamation of waste lands, or to propose a vote

[7] Hansard, vol. xxv. n.s. p. 1117.

of money, and so afford even temporary relief.
Mr. Grattan was supported in his appeal by Mr.
Spring Rice, who pressed the Government to deal
with the question of waste lands. The great
difficulty, he said, which stood in the way of the
cultivation of those lands was caused by the want
of legislative measures, to remove the obstacles
which existed and hindered local effort. However,
the efforts of Mr. Grattan and Mr. Spring Rice
were unavailing. Sir Robert Peel replied, that, it
was not the intention of the Government to propose a vote of money, and upon the subject of
waste lands, he remained altogether silent. Sir
Robert said, that, from his experience of Ireland,
he never saw any permanent good effected by
votes of public money. I believe that the experience of Sir Robert Peel has been the experience
of many other statesmen. It is certainly justified
by history. No permanent good has ever been
effected in the case of Ireland by eleemosynary
legislation. Such legislation demoralizes more
than it relieves. But the demand of the Irish
members was not merely for eleemosynary aid.
They wanted honourable employment for the
people, and they pointed to the direction from
which that employment might come, with permanent advantage to the country. But nothing
was done. The session glided away, and no

measures were passed to save the country from the "famine" which, in the words of Earl Stanhope, "threatened it." Another select committee was, however, appointed. There was no dearth of select committees and of Coercion Bills at all events. If Irish grievances could have been removed by either there would be no land question to-day. But

> " Non tali auxilio nec defensoribus istis."

Sir James Graham once well said, "Violence is not the policy for governing Ireland."[8] And though select committees have their uses, yet they cannot supply the powers and functions of a legislative body.

The report of this committee bears date July 18, 1830. It repeats the old story of misery and want. A considerable portion of the population, nearly one-fifth, it was said, were out of employment, and a condition of poverty and suffering which "no language can possibly describe, and which it is necessary to witness in order fully to estimate," was laid bare. The report dwells at much length on the "law and practice of landlord and tenant," and directs attention to the various suggestions,—such as emigration, the prosecution of public works, and the reclamation of waste lands —which had been made from time to time for

---

[8] *Annual Register*, 1844, p. 59.

remedying the existing disorders. The committee felt that something ought to be done by the Government to meet the exigencies of the crisis. "Your committee conceives," says the report, "that it is the imperative duty of individuals, of the legislature, and of the Government, to consider what means can be devised to diminish the mass of sufferings, and, at the same time, to secure for the country a better economic condition, promoting the better management of estates, and regulating the relation of landlord and tenant on rational and useful principles." The committee concludes their report upon this branch of the inquiry as follows : —"Your committee cannot close this branch of the inquiry, without calling the particular attention of the house to the satisfactory results, stated to have been attained, at Glenbeigh, the estate of Lord Headley. In that experiment there has been shown an example worthy of imitation by other landed proprietors. On this property the problem already referred to has been solved, and an estate has been brought from a wretched condition, equally to the advantage of the landlord, advancing and securing, at the same time, the tenant's prosperity and well-being."

The facts of this case are interesting and important. Lord Headley possessed an estate of some 13,000 acres in one of the wildest and least fertile parts of the County Kerry. In 1807 the population of Glenbeigh was, in the testimony of Mr. Wiggins, the agent of Lord Headley, described as " extremely wild and savage." The district was an asylum for criminals and offenders of all classes. "It was the boast of the people," says Mr. Wiggins, "that no criminal was ever punished from the district." In fact, the king's writ scarcely ran in Glenbeigh. It may well be supposed that where there was so much lawlessness, there was much poverty and want. Indeed, the condition of the people was wretched to the last degree. "Their habitations," says Mr. Wiggins, " were very miserable, the very lowest kind of huts that are to be found in Ireland, without windows or chimneys, and perfectly miserable cabins of the worst kind." There were no roads in the neighbourhood, and apparently but few marks of civilization at all. In fine, Glenbeigh in 1807, and for some years afterwards, was little short of a wild waste inhabited by a poverty-stricken and lawless population. But in 1830 all this was changed. The miserable huts and cabins had disappeared, and neat houses, "as neat as you would find in England," had taken their place. The agriculture of the district had been greatly improved ; and, in fact, a peaceable, industrious, and prosperous people flourished, where not many years before misery and lawlessness prevailed. "By what means was this change effected?" Mr. Wiggins was asked by the committee. He replied : "By attention to the character of the people, and a constant desire on the part of the managers of the estate to avail themselves of the disposition of the people to the improvement of the lands, and to the improvement of their habits and character generally; it was done with very little sacrifice of rent or of money, but a constant and earnest attention to the object of improving the estate by the industry of the people ; and when any particular instance of good management, or industry, or care to collect the sand or weeds, or to reclaim or improve the land, or to build a decent house was evinced by the people, they were encouraged by some little emolument, or attention, or something of the kind. I think the first system was to allow the people half the value of any improvements made, out of the rent ; but as those rents were very considerably higher than could have been paid, we conceived that the allowance was rather nominal than real, though it had the real effect of improving the estate."

"Has there been any improvement in the conduct and character of the people?" Mr. Wiggins was further asked. He answered, "Yes, very considerable improvement ;" adding that, " during the disturbances which had recently occurred in the

country, the spirit of whiteboyism did not extend to
Glenbeigh ;" on the contrary, the inhabitants had
held a meeting, at which resolutions were passed "in
a style rather of.superiority, disowning any participation in those feelings, and stating that the reason
they did not participate in those feelings was the
attention which had been paid to them and their
improvement for so many years."[9] Unhappily the
example of Lord Headley was not imitated by
many other landowners in Ireland. Meanwhile,
Parliament left the tenants to shift for themselves.
No measures were taken to oblige the landlords
to discharge the duties which they neglected, or
to respect the rights which they ignored. Absenteeism continued unchecked, and the improvements
made by the tenants remained unacknowledged.
Thus was their industry discouraged, fettered, and
restrained. The Report of 1830 went the way of all
such reports. Honour to the men who laboured on
those committees. They, at least, did their duty.
They spared no exertion in collecting materials
to enable Parliament to understand and to deal
with the case of landlord and tenant in Ireland ;
but their reports might as well have been un-

[9] *Vide* Report of Select Committee, House of Commons, on the state of the poor in Ireland, 1830, pp. 4
and 9; and Minutes of Mr. Wiggins' evidence, Q. 4033 to
4068.

written, their energies and industry untaxed. Parliament was immovable.

The Session of 1829—30 closed without the adoption of any legislative measures for adjusting the relation of landlord and tenant on " rational and useful principles."

In the speech from the Throne, on the reassembling of Parliament in November, 1830, nothing was said as to the introduction of remedial measures. Reference was, however, made to the discontent prevailing in the country. But the policy foreshadowed in the royal speech for removing this discontent was not a policy of concession, or indeed, of consideration, but of coercion.

"I am determined," says the sovereign, " to exert, to the utmost of my power, all the means which the law and the constitution have placed at my disposal for the punishment of sedition, and for the prompt suppression of outrage and disaffection." Sedition should, indeed, have been suppressed, and outrage and disaffection put down, but a policy of mere coercion was not sufficient for that purpose. England had not learned this lesson in 1830, or indeed for many years afterwards.[1] In the debate upon the address the condition of Ireland formed the principal theme for discussion.

[1] " A government to be loved must be feared," said Lord Stanley in 1833.. *Annual Register*, 1833, p. 18.)

Matters had gone from bad to worse during the recess. The people who, in the first instance, had endeavoured to bear their sufferings and deprivations with fortitude and equanimity, now, despairing apparently of redress, became seditious and turbulent.

Riots had occurred in many parts of the country, and serious collisions had taken place between the peasantry and the police. A very grave state of affairs had, in fact, arisen. The Government, however, seemed unable to realize the condition of things. It was, apparently, the opinion of the Duke of Wellington that the landlords were much to blame for the poverty and distress of the people. " If," said he, " persons of estate and property in Ireland would live there, and spend their incomes in it, they would do more to tranquillize the country than all the measures which his Majesty's Government could adopt." [2] There was a great deal of truth in this, but what if the landlords would not live in the country? The Prime Minister was clearly not of opinion that means ought to be taken to oblige them to live amongst the people, or to enable the people to live without them.

He would not accept Mr. Henry Grattan's suggestion to impose an absentee tax, nor Mr.

[2] Hansard, 3rd series, vol. i. p. 51.

Brownlow's proposal of the reclamation of waste lands. No pressure whatever was put upon the landowners to induce them to amend their ways, although it was evident that they would never amend them of their own accord. It is said, that, when the first Napoleon heard that the Duke of Richmond claimed the territory of Aubigné, the great Corsican observed, " He may have it, if he lives there." But the Iron Duke was not prepared to submit a similar alternative to the landlords of Ireland.

Dire distress now spread throughout Ireland. In the west the pinches of poverty were more especially felt. Famine raged in Mayo, and misery prevailed in all parts.

In December, 1830, Mr. Callaghan, member for Cork city, presented a petition from his constituents praying that the Government would advance funds to enable some of their number to emigrate.[3] But no funds were granted. No steps whatever were taken in the matter.

In February, 1831, Mr. Smith O'Brien moved for leave to bring in a bill for the relief of the "aged, helpless, and infirm poor ;" but Lord Althorp replied that it would not be fair to hold out any hope that the measure could become law.[4]

[3] Hansard, 3rd series, vol. ii. p. 115.

[4] Hansard, 3rd series, vol. ii. p. 246. A bill of a similar character was, however, passed later on in the session.

Mr. Hume at this time attacked the ministry for their coercive Irish policy.[5] Alluding, in a special manner, to the promise of conciliation which they had made when in opposition,[6] but which they did not keep when in power.

On the 18th February, Mr. Browne stated, in the House, that the parish priest of Kilmore, in the Barony of Erris, in the County Mayo, had written him to say that before the end of the month there would be 30,000 people in that district without food. This statement of Mr. Browne was, in its substantial features, corroborated by the Irish Secretary Mr. Stanley. Mr. Stanley said that, from all the inquiries he had made, distress prevailed in Erris to a degree little short of famine. He read a petition he had received from the inhabitants of a place called Tyrawley, in which the petitioners presented a most pitiable and melancholy picture of the condition of things ; stating how, by the decline of the linen trade in their neighbourhood, they had been left dependent on the soil, which now failed to yield them means for subsistence. "Give us," concluded the prayer of the petition, "but the means of maintaining our wives and families, we shall be thankful, we shall be industrious, we shall be happy." "Severe,"

[5] Hansard, vol. ii. 3rd series, p. 331.
[6] Hansard, vol. ii. 3rd series, p. 674.

said Mr. Stanley, "as are the sufferings of those people, their representation of their distress does not contain one syllable of insubordination, or even of discontent," and "for this reason," he added, "it is doubly deserving of the attention of Parliament."

Much of the prevailing distress was, according to Mr. Stanley, attributable to the landlords. They had not, he said, come forward as they ought. He had been furnished with a statement of the rental of one of the baronies he had named. It amounted to 10,400*l.* a year, and out of that large rental only 100*l.* had been contributed to the relief of this distress. Of this sum 70*l.* had been subscribed by non-residents, and 30*l.* by a constant absentee. Mr. Stanley referred, in harsh terms, to the landlords, saying that the local subscription to the distress was trifling, whilst the rents in general were high, and exacted to the uttermost farthing. He concluded his speech by stating that Government were considering a plan to meet the existing condition of things.

Peel, upon the same occasion, alluded to the temperate appeals of the people, but feared no adequate means of relief could be afforded by the Government. The case, he thought, was one, not for Government interference, but for "individual

E

charity and general sympathy." This observation
of the great statesman as to "general sympathy"
reminds me of a story which I once heard of
an eminent judge. He had been trying a case
which had lasted an unusually long time, and
involved very intricate and important matters
for consideration and decision. At the termination of the trial, the jury—a special one—asked
for more than the ordinary fees, on account
of the loss of time, and the excessive trouble to
which they had been subjected. But the judge
replied, "that it was not in his power to help
them, he could not order them more than the
law and the usual practice allowed." "But my
lord," said the foreman, "our case is a very hard
one. We have sustained great losses by being
kept away from our business all this time. A few
days ago another jury made a similar application
to Baron B——, and he said that he felt the
greatest sympathy for them." "Oh," said the
learned judge, "we have misunderstood each
other. I thought it was money, not sympathy, you
wanted. If it is only sympathy, then I can give
you quite as much of *that* as Baron B —— could."
It was not "sympathy" which the Irish people
wanted. Nor was it money, in the eleemosynary
sense of the word. They wanted employment.
They wanted means of earning a decent living

in the land of their fathers. Those means the Government could have placed, yet did not place, within their reach. " But," it has often been said to me by fair-minded Englishmen, " the fault is not with the Government, it is with your own land-lords." I answer, They are not our own landlords. They are your landlords. England forced her land system and her landlords upon Ireland. Upon her then devolved the responsibility of taking heed that this system should work no mischief to the country, and that the men and their descendants whom she has raised to power and wealth, would discharge the duties of the position they owed to her favour. If the question of Irish land tenure had been left for adjustment between the Anglo-Irish landlords and the Irish people, it would have been settled long ago. The landlords would have been compelled to do their duty, or, in the words of a well-known English statesman, they would have been " exterminated by the vengeance of the people." But in the struggles between the Irish people and the landlords, the landlords had England at their back. Her power and arms were used, not in ameliorating the condition of the Irish tenant, but in supporting and maintaining a land system which Mr. Froude has stigmatized as the " most fatal of her gifts " to Ireland. England is originally responsible for establishing and preserving the Irish land system. It is, therefore, impossible to acquit her of all participation in the shortcomings and misdeeds of the Irish landlords, who owe their being as such to English power. I say this, not with the view of opening old wounds, but to point out that the more tardy has been justice to the Irish tenant in the past, the more prompt and complete it ought to be in the present and the future.

Great pressure was now (1831) brought to bear upon the Government to introduce even a temporary measure of relief, and on the 30th March the Chancellor of the Exchequer, Lord Althorp, proposed a vote of 50,000*l.* to be advanced to Commissioners for expenditure on public works in Ireland.

Even as a temporary measure of relief this provision came too late, and was wholly inadequate. But the occasion was not one for temporary measures. Legislation on a bold and statesmanlike scale, and in a spirit of conciliation, was necessary to avert the danger which threatened the very existence of the people. Of the probability of such legislation being adopted there seemed to be no hope. Coercive measures were still the favourite remedies for removing the ills of Ireland, and attaching the people of that country to the British connexion. Though Lord Melbourne had declared, on the 18th March, 1831, that all the witnesses, Catholic and Protestant, magistrates and others, who were examined before various Select Committees, with reference to Ireland, had, with one voice, ascribed the disturbed state of the country to the relations subsisting between landlord and tenant to the manifest injury of both, yet the Government, instead of striking at the root of the disease thus pointed out, persisted in the application of local remedies, which created a great deal of irritation, and did no good.[7]

I think it was Lord Palmerston who once said to a distinguished foreigner who complained of the liberty of discussion allowed in England, that if he were on board a steamship, and if difficulties or fears arose by reason of any very great high steam pressure, the last place, in such an emergency, upon which he would elect to sit would be the safety valve. England continued to sit for a long time upon the political safety valve in Ireland. On the 2nd July, 1831, an Arms Bill was introduced by Mr. Stanley. This bill is known as Stanley's Arms Act. " Elated with the success of the elections, and misled by his law advisers, Mr. Stanley introduced, on the 2nd of July, a bill limiting in Ireland the privilege of having firearms, and punishing their retention in a manner unprecedented in

7 Hansard, vol. iii. 3rd series, p. 524.

any part of the kingdom. Not only the Irish members, Whig and Catholic, and the whole body of the English and Scotch radicals, but even some of his colleagues on the Treasury Bench disapproved of his proposals; his exposition of the measure was listened to with amazement not to be concealed. The Cabinet had some weeks previously acceded to his recommendation, that the existing Arms Act should be renewed for three years, but he subsequently adopted a variety of suggestions rendering the law more stringent and penal, and these he proceeded to embody in the bill, without consulting the Home Secretary [Lord Melbourne], or any other member of the Government. Althorp, writing confidentially to his father [Earl Spencer] on the following day, says, " I did not know that he had altered the bill, and had made it one of the most tyrannical measures I ever heard proposed. I was quite astonished, and so was Graham, for not one of us had ever heard that these alterations were to be made in it. We must stand by Stanley, but we must soften down his measure. It is a great scrape, for O'Connell will have the credit of forcing upon us any modification which is embodied in the bill." [8]

The bill was ultimately softened down, whoever

[8] *Vide* McCullagh Torrens' " Life of Melbourne," vol. i. pp. 370, 371.

deserves credit for it ; no doubt O'Connell from without, and Lord Melbourne from within the Cabinet.

Attention was now directed to the working of the Sub-Letting Act. Lord Melbourne, with that genuine concern for the welfare of the Irish people which characterized all his public efforts, gave great consideration to the appeals and suggestions which were made at the time for the purpose of repealing or amending this Act.

The chief blot in the Sub-Letting Act, and in the disfranchising clauses of the Catholic Relief Bill was that, whilst both measures afforded facilities, or supplied motives to landlords for clearing their estates, no provisions were made for the protection or security of the unfortunate tenants who were thus cast helplessly upon the world. The Sub-Letting Act, in addition, had an *ex-post-facto* effect, which acted injuriously upon the interests of the middlemen. It would be an ungrateful task now-a-days, or, indeed, at any time, to attempt a defence of this class, or to mitigate the censure which posterity has pronounced upon them. But it must not be forgotten that the middlemen owed their existence to the landlords' dereliction of their duties. Had the landlords lived amongst their people, and exhibited such a desire for their well-being as, for instance, Lord Headley had evinced, the evils of "middlemanism" would never have grown up.

"Middlemanism" was a result of landlord non-feasance, and of the general viciousness of the whole law and practice of land tenure in Ireland. That tenure rested upon an irrational, slovenly, and unjust basis. Parliament had not the courage, nor the landlords the desire, to alter it. The tenants alone exhibited a disposition towards improvement.[9] But their efforts were discouraged by the landlords, and not recognized by the Legislature. The middlemen did in a measure what the landlords should have done. They lived in the country. They were the only "gentry" left to guide and elevate, by their example, the peasant and labouring orders. The tenants got something out of them—it was not much ;—"more kicks than halfpence," I fear—but they got nothing out of the

[9] "The landlords," says Mr. Nassau Senior, "are unwilling or unable to expend money on their estates. They allow the tenants themselves to make the provision by building, and by reclaiming land from its original state of bog or heather or stony field. It is thus that many estates have been created, and almost all have been enlarged by generation after generation of tenants without assistance. It was the tenants who made the Barony of Ferney—originally worth 3000*l.*—worth 50,000*l.* a-year."—Mr. Senior, as quoted by Mr. O'Connor Morris (the *Times* special commissioner), in his "Letters on the Irish Land Question," p. 117.

landlords. The Sub-Letting Act had the twofold effect of clearing off both the tenants and the middlemen.[1] The property of the middlemen had, by its operation, become depreciated and less secure, and the result of this depreciation and insecurity was reflected upon the position of the sub-tenant in the way of additionally exorbitant rent leading to increased arbitrary evictions. When Lord Melbourne (then Mr. Lamb) had been in Ireland as Chief Secretary in 1827, his attention was called to the unfair character and injurious operation of the Sub-Letting Act. He fully admitted the inconsiderate and improvident rigour of certain of its provisions, and was disposed to advise its amendment.[2] However, he retired from office shortly afterwards, and nothing further was done until 1831. Lord Melbourne then returned to the subject. He always felt that something besides the introduction of coercion bills ought to be done for the Irish tenant. With a view of learning all that could be learned on the subject, he wrote to Dr. Doyle, the celebrated Bishop of Leighlin, in 1831. "No man," he says, "is more intimately, or practically, acquainted with the state of Ireland than yourself. From your evidence before the Select

[1] *Vide* ante, p. 9.
[2] Torrens' " Life of Melbourne," vol. i. pp. 311, 312.

Committee of 1830, I find that the disposition to
consolidate farms and to eject the poorer tenantry
was encouraged by several enactments, among
which I may specify Sir John Newport's Act, next
the Sub-Letting Act, and afterwards the Act an-
nexed to the late relief bill, which disfranchised
the forty shilling freeholders." Lord Melbourne
now sought to obtain from Dr. Doyle his views as
to the state of affairs created by the working of
those enactments, especially the working of the
Sub-Letting Act.

Dr. Doyle, in reply to the inquiries of the Home
Secretary, " set clearly in moral and political appo-
sition the twofold working of the Sub-Letting Act
as originally passed. *A parte ante* it wrought un-
compensated, and unwarrantable confiscation. *A
parte poste* it might have been a prudential restriction upon the infinitesimal partition of land, but so
long as the rural population had no better employment, or surer chance of subsistence, than the
possession of a potato field, it was idle to expect
them to submit to eviction from their miserable
holdings. Intensely conservative in his love of
order, respect for law, and conviction of the duty of
deference to authority, the patriot bishop deplored
the misery endured by the people, and felt bound
to uplift his voice, stern as that of the prophets
of old, against sordid and shameful oppres-

sion."[3] Lord Melbourne, however, felt himself unable
to interfere with the working of the Act, as far as
it was prospective, but with reference to its retrospective action, he thought a change could be
made. Such a change was accordingly made.
And on the 24th March, 1832, the amended Sub-
Letting Act became law.[4]

The measure had little or no effect, good or ill,
upon the position of the occupiers of the soil. So
far as it conferred any benefits at all, it was the
middlemen who reaped the advantage, by the
elimination of the retrospective clauses. But the
Sub-Letting Acts, original or amended, are scarcely
worth referring to as contributions to remedial
legislation on the Irish land question. They
were, no doubt, intended as remedial measures,
and it was, probably, thought they would so
operate, but neither of them was calculated to
improve, and, as a matter of fact, neither did,
in the slightest degree, improve the condition
of the occupiers of the soil. The first of them
checked sub-letting, while it left the tenant utterly
unprovided for after he had been flung destitute on
the world by its operation. The second redressed
the grievances of the middlemen, but left those
of the sub-tenant untouched. The first excited

---

[3] Torrens' "Life of Lord Melbourne," vol. i. pp. 361, 363.
[4] 2nd and 3rd William IV. c. 17.

great dissatisfaction, the second produced no contentment.

The condition of affairs had now grown
desperate. The people were filled with despair.
Catholic emancipation, from which so much was
expected, had, in fact, accomplished nothing as
to the material, and not much as to the political, condition of the people.   Its primary visible
effects were the disfranchisement of the forty
shilling freeholders.   Electoral privileges had been
narrowed, and religious equality had not been, so
far, realized.   As a measure of religious relief, it
was practically a dead-letter on the statute-book.
"In 1833," says Mr. Lecky, "there was not in
Ireland a single Catholic judge, or stipendiary
magistrate.   All the high sheriffs, with one exception, the overwhelming majority of the unpaid
magistrates, and all the grand jurors, the five
inspectors-general, and the thirty sub-inspectors
of police, were Protestant.   The chief towns were
in the hands of narrow, corrupt, and intensely
bigoted corporations.   Even in a Whig Government, not a single Irishman had a seat in the
Cabinet, and the Irish Secretary was Mr. Stanley,
whose imperious manners and unbridled temper
had made him intensely hated.   For many years
promotion had been steadily withheld from those

who advocated Catholic emancipation, and the majority of the people thus found their bitterest enemies in the foremost places."[b]

Thus, whilst religious disabilities continued virtually unremoved, and whilst the Government measure of emancipation was associated in the minds of the people with the deprivation of electoral rights, the peasantry were sinking under the weight of a land system which could not be defended, but which Parliament obdurately declined to reform.

In 1833 another coercion bill was passed, but nothing more was done to remove the cause of the discontent, which the Government tried vainly to smother. On the 21st July, 1834, Mr. Poulett Scrope made one more effort to persuade the Government to introduce some measure for the protection and security of the Irish tenant, but to no purpose. It will hardly be wondered at, that the people should have now eagerly turned their minds towards the repeal of the Union. In some of the petitions, presented at the time by the Irish peasantry, the English Parliament was earnestly entreated to deal with the question of landlord and tenant, or to restore to Ireland its native legislature. But nothing was done to adjust the relation of

[b] Lecky's " Leaders of Public Opinion in Ireland," p. 260.

landlord and tenant. And as to repeal, the minister declared that even the constitutional expression of a desire for it would be perfectly useless ; in fact, he said that the people of England would resist it to the death. "At the same time," observes Mr. Lecky, "it is scarcely an exaggeration to say that the British Constitution had no existence in Ireland." [6]

[6] Lecky's "Leaders of Public Opinion in Ireland," p. 260.

IV.

1835 TO 1852.

ON the 2nd of July, 1835, Mr. Sharman Crawford, then member for Dundalk, moved for leave to bring in a bill to amend the law of landlord and tenant in Ireland.[1] Hitherto the efforts which had been made to deal with the agrarian problem were chiefly directed to the subject of the reclamation of waste lands. The immediate cause of distress in Ireland was shown to have been the want of employment. It was felt that, if this want could be supplied, a better state of things would quickly ensue. The means for supplying it were close at hand. Thousands of acres of waste land covered the country. Upon works for their reclamation the people might, it was urged, have been employed advantageously to themselves and the country. But capital, and the necessary legislative measures for stimulating and sustaining such works, could not, as we have seen, be obtained. Mr. Sharman Crawford now

[1] Hansard, vol. xxix. 3rd series, p. 218.

made a new departure, and for the first time broached the principle that the tenant was entitled to compensation for his outlay on the land. This bill was what we should now call a very modest measure indeed. It proposed that the tenant should be entitled, on eviction, to compensation for improvements of a permanent nature made with the landlord's consent. In certain cases, compensation might, according to this measure, have been awarded for improvements made without the consent of the landlord, provided they were such as the actual wants of the tenant required. It was to be left to the chairman of quarter sessions to decide in what cases the tenant would be entitled to compensation for improvements made without the consent of the landlord.[2]

Mr. Crawford, in now moving for leave to bring in his bill, explained that it was not his intention, owing to the state of public business, to press the measure forward that session, but that he would introduce the subject again next year. Meanwhile, honourable members would have time to consider his proposal.

In 1836, on the 10th March, Mr. Crawford accordingly reintroduced his bill. Upon this occasion

[2] Hansard, 3rd series, vol. xxix. p. 218, and vol. xxxii. p. 186.

he went more at length into the subject, referring to the reports of the various committees to which I have made allusion, and quoting from the evidence of impartial witnesses like Mr. Nimmo, Sir F. Lewis, and Mr. Leslie Foster, in support of his demand for prompt legislation on the subject. He pleaded, he said, the cause of the wretched, starving, rack-rented tenantry of Ireland, whose habitations were unfit for human beings, and whose land was in the most deficient state of cultivation. All he now claimed, and he believed that the remedy would be an effectual one, was that some means should be given to the tenant for obtaining compensation for the fruits of his toil and labour when he was ejected from the soil on which they were expended.

The representatives of the landlords in the House of Commons opposed this very moderate measure. Colonel Connolly denounced it as an unjustifiable interference with the rights of property, and Mr. Lefroy took the unusual course of resisting even the motion for leave to bring in the bill. There were two landlords in the House, however, who supported Mr. Crawford's appeal— Mr. Poulett Scrope and Mr. William Smith O'Brien. Leave was given to bring in the bill, but it never reached another stage.

Finding that Mr. Crawford had been unsuccessful

F

in his efforts, Mr. Lynch, another Irish member, returned to the old question of waste lands, and on the 12th December, 1837, asked for leave to bring in a bill on that ancient subject. But his efforts were not more successful than Mr. Crawford's of the previous year had been.

The period at which we have now arrived was unquestionably one of exceptionable disturbance and distress ; but then, as at all times before and since, the disturbances and distractions which prevailed were mainly, if not entirely, attributable to the unfortunate relation of landlord and tenant.

Lord Mulgrave, addressing the House of Lords in November, 1837, and referring to certain statements which had been made to the effect that agrarian outrages originated in religious feuds, said, " I have the authority of many who attended the assizes for stating that, according to their belief, no such thing takes place in Ireland as the murder of a man on account of his religion. A man happens to be murdered as a part of that dreadful system of combination which exists in Ireland with regard to the tenure of land. It is merely a coincidence that he happens to be a Protestant."[3]

In 1842 a commencement of practical legislation on the subject of waste lands, which, as a preliminary phase of the land question, had been

[3] *Annual Register*, 1838, p. 97.

brought almost continuously under the notice of Parliament since the Union, was at last made. In August of that year the Irish Arterial Drainage Act was passed. The measure, however, proved ineffectual until it was amended by the Summary Proceedings Act of 1846. I shall state the effect of these measures in the words of Mr. John George McCarthy, who has in a special manner devoted himself to a subject which it is impossible altogether to pass over in any work upon the land question.

" These measures," says Mr. McCarthy, " enabled the Board of Works, as a department of the State, to undertake the great national work of arterial drainage, charging the cost on the land improved. Vigorous efforts were made to take advantage of this legislation—landlords and tenants worked together. Every county, almost every barony, made its proposals. Four hundred and fifty-two districts were surveyed ; 122 districts, comprising 270,000 acres, were reclaimed. Of the remaining districts, 300 were under consideration, and it was estimated that ten years would complete them. But in the midst of the work came the famine, and since then the great national work of arterial drainage has been at a stand-still."[4]

The Drainage Act of 1842 was followed by a

[4] Mr. McCarthy's Letter to the *Times,* Oct. 28, 1819.

more important step. Sir Robert Peel, yielding to the importunities of Mr. Sharman Crawford, consented in 1843 to the appointment of a Royal Commission to inquire into the question of the "occupation of land in Ireland." This commission is popularly known as the Devon Commission. Its appointment marks an important epoch in the history of the land question. The commission sat for two years. Its members, presided over by an English landlord, the Earl of Devon, were indefatigable in their efforts and zealous in their anxiety to probe to the core the great cause of Ireland's misery and discontent. The result of their inquiries and deliberations was the collection of fresh evidence, in corroboration of that already before Parliament, tending to prove that the source of all Ireland's misfortunes and poverty was the fatal system of land-tenure existing in the country. Of the condition of the people the commissioners write :—

"A reference to the evidence of most of the witnesses will show that the agricultural labourer of Ireland continues to suffer the greatest privations and hardships ; that he continues to depend upon casual and precarious employment for subsistence ; that he is badly housed, badly fed, badly clothed, and badly paid for his labour. Our personal experience and observations during our inquiry have afforded us a melancholy confirmation of these statements, and we cannot forbear expressing our strong sense of the patient endurance which the labouring classes have generally exhibited under sufferings greater, we believe, than the people of any other country in Europe have to sustain."[1]

The great means for bettering the condition of the peasantry, the commissioners point out, "are an increased and improved cultivation of the soil," to be effected by securing for the tenant, through legislative enactments, "fair remuneration for the outlay of his capital and labour."

"Although it is certainly desirable," says the report, "that the fair remuneration to which a tenant is entitled for his outlay of capital or of labour, in permanent improvements, should be secured to him by voluntary agreement rather than by compulsion of law ; yet, upon a review of all the evidence furnished to us upon the subject, we believe that some legislative measure will be found necessary in order to give efficacy to such agreements, as well as to provide for those cases which cannot be settled by private arrangement. We earnestly hope that the Legislature will be disposed to entertain a bill of this nature, and to pass it into law with as little delay as is consistent with a full discussion of its principles and details."

[1] "Digest of Devon Commission," vol. ii. p. 1116.

" We are convinced that, in the present state of feelings in Ireland, no single measure can be better calculated to allay discontent, and to promote substantial improvement throughout the country. In some case, the existence of such a law will incline the landlord to expend his own capital in making permanent improvements. In others, he may be called upon, on the eviction or retirement of tenants, to provide the amount for which their claims may be established under the Act."[6]

Lord Devon did not think that the duties under-taken by him for the purpose of attempting the solution of the land question had terminated when the report of the commissioners was presented. He knew how unproductive of practical results similar reports and inquiries had been, and he was resolved that the commission with which his name is so honourably associated should not, if he could help it, be a failure. On the 6th of May, 1845, he presented a number of petitions, and supported their prayers with his voice and influence. The

---

[6] Report of Commission appointed to inquire into the occupation of land in Ireland, Feb. 14, 1845. The Devon Commission was composed exclusively of landlords; 303 witnesses were examined—47 landlords, 47 agents, 128 farmers, and 81 not classed. Fifty-five witnesses said that the best way to encourage tenants to improve was to give them leases, and 146 to give them fair compensation for improvement.

petitioners begged that some measure might be introduced into Parliament for securing to industrious tenants the benefits which were derived from the improvements they had made upon the land. "If some measure of this kind," said his lordship, "were passed, it would much strengthen the industry of the people of Ireland."

Lord Stanley, in reply, said that every one must feel the importance of the recommendation, and added that nothing "went so much to the root of the social condition of the people of Ireland as the providing greater security to the industrious tenant of some compensation for the permanent, or almost permanent, improvements effected by him during his occupation of the land." Lord Stanley concluded by expressing a hope that some such measure would be brought forward by the Government on an early day.[7]

Faithful to his promise, Lord Stanley, on June 9th, 1845, introduced a bill for "the purpose of providing compensation to tenants in Ireland, in certain cases, on being dispossessed of their holdings, for such improvements as they may have made during their tenancy."

The bill proposed that tenants should be entitled to compensation, on disturbance, for prospective improvements of a permanent nature, made with

[7] Hansard, vol. lxxx. 3rd series, pp. 225 and 227.

the consent of the landlord ; or, without his consent, provided the improvements had been effected
with the authority and approval of a commissioner
of improvements, to be specially appointed for the
purpose. The functions of the commissioner were
to inspect the lands, and to examine and inquire
whether they would "bear" improvement; and
then, if he thought well of it, to authorize the
works contemplated by the tenant, and to award,
in case of eviction, such measure of compensation
as was deemed fair and equitable.

Lord Stanley's speech in introducing this measure
was one of the most valuable contributions rendered
to the subject of land tenure in Ireland up to
that date, and it has a living interest to-day.

Having dwelt upon the wretched condition of
the country as exposed by the Devon commission,
and rejected the ancient nostrum for all the ills of
Ireland—emigration—his lordship pointed out how
different were the incidents and circumstances of
the relation of landlord and tenant in Ireland as
compared to the incidents and circumstances of
that relation in England ; and wound up a speech,
which must ever be remembered for its powerful
advocacy of the cause of the Irish tenant, by
urging, that the land question was to be solved
by rooting the occupier not out of, but in the soil.
" The remedy for the evils of Ireland," said Lord

Stanley, "is not emigration, but a system under which the tenant would be induced to invest his labour and capital in the land."[8]

The bill was opposed by the Irish landlords, led by Lord Clanricarde and the Marquis of Londonderry.

Their chief objection was to the clauses enabling the commissioner of improvements to step in between them and the tenants, and to authorize improvements which they would not allow. Of course the bill, without those clauses, would be a perfect nullity. If the industrious tenant who wished to improve were to suspend his operations until he should receive the consent of the landlord, then he would, in all probability, wait until the crack of doom. On the other hand, if he were to improve without that consent, then the fruits of his labour and capital would be confiscated, as they had ever been.[9]

[8] Hansard, June 9, 1845, vol. lxxxi. 3rd series, p. 211. (*Vide* Appendix B.)

[9] "It is well known that in England and in Scotland, before a landlord offers a farm for letting, he finds it necessary to provide a suitable farm-house, with necessary farm-buildings, for the proper management of the farm. He puts the gates and fences into good order, and he takes upon himself a great part of the burden of keeping the buildings in repair during the term ; and the rent is fixed with reference to this state of things. Such, at least, is generally the case, although special contracts may occasionally be made, vary-

The bill was, however, read a first time on this day.

On June 24th it came on for the second reading. The representatives of the Irish landlords in the House of Peers opposed it vigorously. The bill was, however, read a second time against a solemn protest signed by the following dissentient peers: — Lords Monteagle and Brandon, Gosford, Campbell, Chaworth (Meath), Crofton, Charlemount, Lismore, Somerhill (Clanricarde), Kinard and Rosse, Carew, Clanbrassil (Roden), Lucan, Charleville, Stradbroke, Massarene, Sandwich, Rosse, Lorton, Egmont, Kingston, Londonderry.

ing the arrangement between landlord and tenant. In Ireland the case is wholly different. . . . In most cases [there] whatever is done in the way of building or fencing is done by the tenant ; and, in the ordinary language of the country, dwelling-houses, farm-buildings, and even the making of fences, are described by the general word 'improvements,' which is thus employed to denote the necessary adjuncts, without which, in England or in Scotland, no tenant would be found to rent it." ("Report of the Devon Commission Digest," vol. ii. pp. 1122—1123.)

Mr. O'Connor Morris (the *Times* special commissioner), writing in 1868-9 observes, upon the law as to improvement :—"In Ireland, where in most cases what is done in the way of improving the soil is done by the tenant, not by the landlord, and where the tenant in the majority of instances has not risen to the *status* of a free contractor, the law is in the highest degree unfair ; it refuses to protect what really is the property of the tenant, added to the holding, and exposes it to unredressed confiscation." (Letters to the *Times*, p. 148.)

On the 26th June Lord Stanley, who certainly seems to have pushed the bill with vigour and persistency, moved for the appointment of a select committee to consider the measure, and upon this committee Lord Clanricarde indignantly refused to serve.[1]

Lord Stanley apparently did what he could, but the opposition which he had to encounter was too strong even for him.

On the 15th July he abandoned the bill in consequence of the strong feeling manifested against it by the select committee and the House.[2]

Two days afterwards, Sharman Crawford, finding that Lord Stanley had failed, moved for leave to bring in a Tenant Right Bill, which he had intended introducing in 1843, but had subsequently withdrawn to await the result of the Devon Commission and the action of the Government thereupon. But the member for Rochdale could scarcely hope to succeed where a Cabinet minister had failed. Indeed, he had little or no hope of an immediate settlement, but he was determined that the question should be kept before Parliament and the country. He trusted, with the sanguine temperament of an earnest and honest man, that members might, perhaps, study the bill during

[1] Hansard, July 26, 1845.
[2] Hansard, July 15, 1845.

the recess, and thus become interested in the question, and more capable of discussing and considering it on the reassembling of Parliament. The session now passed away, and nothing was effected for the Irish tenant. The recommendations of the Devon Commission were not carried out. The Irish landlords were too strong. The House of Lords was too obstructive.

On the assembling of Parliament the next year, 1846, Mr. Crawford again returned to the charge, and on the 16th February asked Sir Robert Peel if it was the intention of Her Majesty's Government to deal with the Irish land question that session, but the Prime Minister replied, "he feared not." The experience of the previous session was not encouraging. However, despite the unpromising answer of Sir R. Peel, another attempt was made by the Government, on the 11th June following, to settle the question.[3] Earl Lincoln, then Chief Secretary for Ireland, introduced on this day "a bill for providing compensation in certain cases for tenants in Ireland who shall build on, or drain farms, and to secure to the parties respectively entitled thereto due payment for such improvements." This bill was substantially the same as Lord Stanley's of the previous year, substituting the Assistant Barrister as a Court of Reference instead

[3] Hansard, 3rd series, vol. viii. p. 279.

of " a Commissioner of Improvements " appointed
under the latter measure.

Mr. Sharman Crawford gave his support to this
bill, expressing at the same time his regret that it
was not retrospective in its application. It passed ·
through the first reading, but the ministry, having
been defeated in a discussion on the Arms
(Ireland) Bill on the 29th June, resigned, and so
the matter terminated.

A Liberal Ministry, with Lord John Russell
at its head, came into power on the 6th July,
1846, and sanguine hopes were entertained in
Ireland, as to the probabilities of prompt and
effective legislation being now adopted on the land
question.

Those hopes were not immediately realized.
The Government seemed disposed to inactivity, or
at all events, to tardiness. Mr. Sharman Crawford
observing this, asked for leave on the 25th February, 1847, to bring in a bill " to secure the rights of
occupying tenants in Ireland, and thereby promote
the improvement of the soil, and the employment
of the labouring classes."[4]

He explained, in a brief speech, that the object
of the measure was to extend to the rest of Ireland
the system of Tenant Right which prevailed in the
north, and which had done so much to promote

[4] Hansard, 3rd series, vol. x. p. 502.

the prosperity and contentment of the agricultural population in that part of the country. Leave was given, and on the 28th April the bill came on for the second reading.

Mr. Bernal Osborne moved its rejection, protesting against the extension of the Ulster custom to the other parts of the country. Such little interest did the Government apparently take in the subject at this time, though they had turned out the Tories on an Irish issue, that not a member of the Cabinet was present during the discussion. Indeed, her Majesty's Ministers were solely represented upon the occasion by the Irish Solicitor-General of the day, Mr. Monahan, at whose suggestion the debate was adjourned. It was resumed on the 16th June, when the bill was rejected by a majority of 87— 112 to 25.[*]

In the following year, Sir William Somerville, Irish Secretary, brought in a bill, which was nothing more nor less than a transcript of the Earl of Lincoln's bill.

The principle of both measures was identical, but an alteration was now made in the machinery. An Arbitrator was to be appointed under Sir William Somerville's bill for authorizing the im-

---

[*] The following Irish landlords voted for the bill : Viscount Castlereagh, Sir H. W. Barron, Mr. Poulet Scrope. (Hansard, 3rd series, vol. xcvi. p. 630.)

provements, in place of the Assistant Barrister suggested by Earl Lincoln.

Mr. Sharman Crawford intimated his desire to support the Government bill, but he feared that it might have the effect of undermining the Ulster custom, and for this reason :—

The principle of the bill (and its operation was not limited to the south) substantially was, that the consent of the landlord should be a condition precedent to enable the tenant to recover compensation for improvements. But in Ulster, the custom had been that the tenant, if disturbed, for any cause whatever, was entitled (to adopt the language of Mr. Crawford) to go before a legal tribunal, and, proving the value of the property created by his labour (whether the landlord consented or not), to claim compensation according to the value resulting therefrom.

There was one other grave blot in this bill adverted to by Mr. Crawford. It was not retrospective in its operation.

Mr. Crawford and the Irish members, however, though not liking the bill very much, offered no serious opposition to it. In fact, they were glad to get anything in the shape of a measure to amend the law and practice of landlord and tenant. The bill was read a first time on the 16th February, 1848, without a discussion. However, the Tenant

Right question was now well started. Attention
had been called to the Ulster custom, and the
tenant farmers of Munster, Leinster, and Connaught began to feel, and to argue in homely
phraseology, that what was " sauce for the goose
ought to be sauce for the gander."

If, it was contended, the agricultural population
of Ulster had become prosperous and contented
under the land system of Ulster, why not extend
that system to the other provinces ? Certainly, the
experiment was at all events worth trying, it was
said. Such being the popular view, it is unnecessary to say that Mr. Crawford found himself
unable, even if he was disposed, to abandon his
Tenant Right Bill for the Government measure.
He accordingly pushed it on simultaneously
with Sir William Somerville's proposal. He
had withdrawn his bill of 1843 to make way for
the Government measure ; but what had then
taken place did not encourage him to act similarly
now. Moreover, the country was in a less conciliatory spirit in 1848 than it had been in 1843.

On the 8th March, Mr. Crawford asked for
leave to bring in his Tenant Right Bill, and
it came on for second reading on the 22nd of the
month.

Mr. Crawford urged that the simplest way to
solve the Irish land question was, not by intro-

ducing new laws and customs into the country, but
by firmly establishing and extending an old
custom already existing there and working
well.

Mr. Trelawney moved the rejection of the bill,
denouncing it as a measure of " confiscation."

Sir William Somerville also opposed it, admitting, however, that the Ulster custom was a
" good custom," but asserting, without explaining
very clearly his meaning, that it would be a "bad
law." He felt, manifestly, that it would be well if
the landlords throughout the country permitted the
custom to exist, but he apparently thought that
no legal compulsion should be placed upon them
to do so. The tenants, Sir William was doubtless
of opinion, should be left dependent on the good-
ness of the landlords, and he probably thought
that if the latter were wise they would be good ;
but in his estimation no steps ought to be taken to
make the tenant independent of the landlord, if he
happened to be a bad one. This, I think, is the
argument which might fairly be deduced from the
observations of the Irish Secretary.[6]

The debate was adjourned to the 5th April,
when Mr. Crawford's bill was defeated by a majority of 145 to 122. Sir William Somerville now
brought forward *his* bill for the second reading.

[6] Hansard, 3rd series, vol. xcvii. p. 863.

G

Mr. Verner moved its rejection, but subsequently withdrew his amendment. The bill was then read a second time, and referred to a select committee. The committee, however, did not report until nearly the end of the session, when it was too late to make any further progress with the measure. But Ireland was not to be left altogether without legislative notice.

On Saturday, the 22nd July, Lord John Russell moved the suspension of the Habeas Corpus Act.[7] The House had assembled specially for the purpose. Mr. Crawford moved, as an amendment, "that the present distracted state of Ireland arises from misgovernment and from want of remedial measures, without which no coercive measures can restore either order or contentment to the country." The amendment was lost by a majority of 271 to 8.[8] The standing orders were then suspended, and the House sat until seven o'clock on Sunday morning to push the measure through. If but a quarter of the energy put forth at this memorable sitting, for the purpose of suspending the constitution in Ireland, had been employed, at any time since the Union, in passing remedial measures for

[7] Hansard, vol. c. p. 696.

[8] The eight were—Messrs. Callaghan, Mr. Devereux, R. M. Fox, J. Greive, F. O'Conor, J. Reynolds, J. Scully, M. Sullivan ; tellers, Mr. Crawford and Mr. Fagan. (Hansard, 3rd series, vol. c. p. 696.)

the country, then it would never have been said, as it was said, even before this date, by Earl Grey, —" Ireland is the one deep blot upon the brightness of British honour;" " Ireland is our disgrace;" " The evils of Ireland could only be produced by misgovernment." [9]

On the 23rd July, 1849, Mr. Horsman moved " that an humble address be presented to her Majesty, praying her to take into her consideration the condition of Ireland." " What have we done for Ireland?" said Mr. Horsman. " Ireland has been truly described as one adjourned debate. We found her prostrate in February; have we raised her in July? Ireland is now entering on the fourth year of famine; sixty per cent. of her population are receiving relief. What are the causes which have produced such results? Bad legislation, careless legislation, criminal legislation, has been the cause of all the disasters we are now deploring." [1]

Mr. Horsman's resolution led to an animated debate—but to nothing else.

On the 18th February, 1850, Sir William Somerville reintroduced his bill, [2] altered to the extent that an " Inspector of Improvements " was

---

[9] Hansard, 3rd series, vol. lxxxiv. p. 1345.
[1] Hansard, July 23, 1849.
[2] Hansard, 3rd series, vol. cviii., p. 1021.

proposed to be appointed, instead of an arbitrator or umpire as at first suggested.

In fact, the Government had practically gone back to Lord Stanley's original proposal for working his bill, for the working of their bill now— viz. the appointment of "a Commissioner of Improvements."

The bill, as altered, was read a second time on the 1st May, and "committed;" but, if I may be forgiven the use of a *legalism*, it was never brought to trial. The Government, in fact, "withdrew from the prosecution." This, I feel bound to say, was the only kind of "prosecution" that the Government ever showed any disinclination to proceed with in the administration of the affairs of Ireland.

On the 10th June, 1850, Mr. Sharman Crawford returned to the charge, and once again endeavoured to push on his Tenant Right Bill, but without success. He got leave to bring it in, but of course the session was too far gone to admit of any further concessions in the matter.

On the 8th April, 1851, Sir H. W. Barron moved for a committee of the whole House " to inquire into the state of Ireland, *and more especially the best means for amending the relationships of landlord and tenant.*" [3]

[3] The words in italics were added to the original resolution on the suggestion of Mr. S. Crawford.

Lord John Russell opposed the resolution, saying that if the law of landlord and tenant needed
amendment, the proper course to take was for
some private member, or for the Government, to
bring in a bill on the subject, not to raise the
question by way of a resolution so vague as the
present.

But Lord John Russell, from that day until he
left office, never introduced a bill on the part of the
Government, or supported a bill introduced by a
private member.

Sir H. W. Barron's resolution was negatived by
a majority of 9—138 to 129.[4]

Seven years had now elapsed since the report
of the Devon Commission was placed before
parliament. That report had recommended the
enactment of legislative measures to protect the
fruits of the tenants' industry in Ireland. The
recommendation was not carried out. No bill was
passed by the Imperial parliament in the interests
of the tenants. But, to use the words of Mr.
Finlason, the able editor of Reeve's " History of
English Law," " an act was passed for the relief of
the *landlords*. This was the Encumbered Estates
Act, which was based upon the policy that had
always been pursued upon the land question of

[4] Mr. Disraeli voted with the minority.

Ireland, the policy of providing rather for the improvement of the *land* than of the people; of promoting speculative purchases and leases for landlords rather than tenants; and often for *absent*, not resident owners."[5]   The Devon Commission

[5] Finlason's "Land Tenure," p. 113, et seq. Mr. Finlason adds, and, as a lawyer, his view of the operation of the Encumbered Estates Act is worth stating :—"Speculative purchasers," he says, "under the Encumbered Estates Court have not scrupled, in the keen pursuit of that pecuniary profit which has been the object of their purchases, to trample even upon the customary tenant right of the north ; so that it is being invaded, disturbed, and endangered; and from this fact it may be inferred what their conduct has been in other districts where such right has not been established. There cannot be a doubt—it has been placed beyond a doubt by the testimony of persons of the highest authority and best acquainted with Ireland—that whatever economical advantages may have been obtained by the operation of the Encumbered Estates Act, it had this great disadvantage, that it vastly augmented that which had for ages been one of the worst evils of Ireland—the conduct of the relation of landlord and tenant upon a commercial principle, making it a mere matter of speculation and of pecuniary profit. These purchases being made, for the most part, for profit, the transfers were carried out so as best to realize profit, and with little regard for tenant right, which, indeed, was not much recognized in those parts of the country in which the transfers took place. The results were wholesale evictions and widespread misery, and a vile commercial spirit in the relation between landlord and tenant. There is a large amount of evidence in the opinion of the most recent and intelligent observers to show that, even in regard to mere material prosperity, the improvement of the land by measures

had declared that something should be done for the tenant. Nothing was done for the tenant, despite the efforts of Lord Devon and those who had participated in his labours. The Devon Commission, like all the commissions and committees which had sat to inquire into the relation of landlord and tenant in Ireland, was so far unproductive of practical results. But the country was now thoroughly roused to action. The question had made way in public opinion, if not in parliament. A great champion had also arisen in England to do battle for the Irish peasantry.

Their cause had, apparently, made little or no impression on parliament, but it had made a great impression on Mr. Bright. He had studied the report and evidence of the Devon Commission with zealous care. He felt for the wrongs of the Irish peasantry. He was determined that justice should be done them, and he now joined with the Irish members in their efforts to obtain a reformation of the Land Laws.

To have won such a champion to their side was a substantial gain for the Irish tenants.

based upon the commercial principle, and which have proceeded upon the consolidation of farms, and the expatriation of the peasantry, has not been greatest."—pp. 114-116.

V.

1852 TO 1869.

"AGITATE, agitate," said the Marquis of Anglesea on one occasion to Daniel O'Connell, "and you will succeed."[1]

An agitation, vigorous and wide-spread, was now raised in the interests of the tenant farmers throughout Ireland. "The sturdy Presbyterians of Down, and Antrim, and Derry were as resolute as the quick-blooded Catholic celts of Cork, Mayo, and Tipperary. For the first time in fifty years, Ulster held out a hand to Munster in fraternal grasp. The ruin which had desolated the other provinces was beginning its work of destruction in the North."[2] Foremost amongst the advocates of Tenant Right were Charles Gavan Duffy, Frederick Lucas, John Francis Maguire, Patrick McMahon, George Henry Moore, and the veteran champion of the cause, Sharman Crawford.

[1] McCullagh Torrens' "Life of Lord Melbourne," vol. i. p. 320.
[2] "New Ireland," 6th ed., p. 143.

On the 10th February, 1852, Mr. Crawford was " up and doing," fighting, apparently, against hope, but determined to stand to his guns, whatever should befall.

He now asked leave to bring in a " Bill for the better securing and regulating the custom of Tenant Right in Ulster, and to secure compensation to improving tenants, who may not claim under the custom, and to limit the power of eviction in certain cases."

The proposal which Mr. Crawford made with reference to regulating the measure of compensation was this :—

That where the tenant claimed compensation, each party should name an arbitrator; the arbitrators to appoint an umpire. If the arbitrators could not agree as to an umpire, or if no award were made, then the question should be left to the decision of the Assistant Barrister in all cases under 100*l.*, and to the Judge of Assize in all cases above that sum.

Sir George Grey, on the part of the Government, said he would not oppose the motion for leave to bring in the bill, but could not hold out any hopes as to the likelihood of its being read a second time. There was one point, however, on which Sir George was clear and decided. He thought that the agitation in Ireland should be put down with the "strong arm." The old remedy. One would have thought that the time had come for abandoning the "strong arm" policy; that it had been weighed in the balance and found wanting. Sir George Grey and the Government were not apparently of this mind. But not so Mr. Bright, who supported the bill, and said he would stand by the Irish members on the vital question of Irish Land. Concession, not coercion, was the policy which the member for Manchester advised. Alluding to the prevailing agitation, the existence of agrarian outrages, and the disturbed condition of the country generally, Mr. Bright said, " It was in the eternal decrees of providence, that so long as the population of a country were prevented from the possibility of possessing any portion of their native soil by legal enactments, and legal chicanery, these outrages should be committed, were they but as beacons and warnings to call the Legislature to a sense of the duties it owed to the country which it governed.[3]

Leave was given to bring in the bill.

Ten days afterwards the Ministry were defeated by a majority of eleven on their Militia Bill, and resigned. Lord Derby took office at the head of a Conservative Government.

On the 31st March, Mr. Crawford's Bill came on

[3] Hansard, 3rd series, vol. cxix. p. 368.

for the second reading Sir Emerson Tennant moved its rejection. The debate which ensued was adjourned to the 5th May, when the bill was defeated by a majority of 167 to 57. Mr. Napier, the Irish Attorney-General, however, took the opportunity of saying in the course of the discussion, that it was the intention of the Government to take up the subject at an early date.

On the 22nd November, Mr. Napier asked and obtained leave to present to the House A new code, for regulating the Relations of Landlord and Tenant in Ireland.

This code, as described by Sergeant (afterwards Justice) Shee, then a leading member of the Irish Parliamentary party, consisted of four Bills :—*A Land Improvement Bill,* by which the tenants for life of settled estates were empowered to charge them with the amount of monies borrowed for their improvement, and to raise, even in the case of leases, in respect of such improvements, the rent of the lands improved.

A *Landlord and Tenant Law Consolidation Bill,* by which a multitude of positive regulations scattered over many Acts of Parliament were amended and reduced to a system, upon the whole calculated, along with suitable encouragements of industry, to promote the true interests of both Landlord and Tenant.

A *Leasing Powers Bill,* by which Landlords whose powers of leasing and agreement were limited by settlement or statutable restriction were enabled to encourage, by leases and agreements for compensation binding upon their successors in estate, the improvements of their lands by the Tenants of them.

And, lastly, a *Tenants' Improvements Compensation Bill,* which, in addition to arrangements securing compensation prospectively to improving tenants, declared, in explicit language, for every kind of agricultural melioration, farm houses, farm buildings suitable to the holding, reclamations of waste lands, clearing away of rocks and stones, draining, fencing, irrigation, tillages, and manurings, the principle, as against an evicting landlord, of *retrospective compensation.*[4]

The first three of those Bills may be described as landlord bills. The last was the tenants' bill.

This measure was certainly a great step in advance. It declared at last in favour of compensation for retrospective improvements. Of the justice of this principle it is unnecessary, I think, to speak. The Irish tenants, as Mr. Lucas once pointed out, were the meritorious cause of the increased value of

---

[4] " Papers, Letters, &c., of Mr. Justice Shee on the Irish Land Question," p. 199, and *vide* Sir Charles Gavan Duffy's speech, *post.*

landed property in Ireland since 1780.[5] To have
limited the operation of any measure introduced for
the tenant's security, to prospective improvements
merely, would be to leave unrecognized and unprotected the rights which the tenants then had
to the property which had been added to the soil
by their capital and industry. Compensation for
prospective improvements was a provision for the
benefit of posterity. "What has posterity done for
us that we should do anything for posterity," said
Sir Boyle Roche. Without being actuated by
the selfish sentiments of the great "Bull" maker
of the Irish Parliament, the Irish tenants thought,
not unfairly or unnaturally, that something should
be done for present as well as for future generations. Indeed, it seemed not altogether impro-
bable, in the then condition of things in the
country, that, if relief did not reach the existing
tenants, there would be no future tenants to relieve.[6] The recognition of the principle of retrospective compensation was essential to the success
of any measure intended to do justice to the
tenants, and to tranquillize the country.

To Mr. Napier belongs the credit of being the

[5] Hansard, Dec. 13, 1852.

[6] "By 1850 the eviction scenes had filled the land with un-
easiness and alarm." "New Ireland," p. 143. Between 1831
and 1861 3,097,415 souls emigrated from Ireland. "Thom's
Official Directory," 1852, pp. 188–9.

first member of a government who braved the hostility and odium of the landlords, by boldly recognizing, and trying to establish by law this principle. The Irish members were, upon the whole, pleased with Mr. Napier's Bill.

They, however, felt that Mr. Crawford's Bill ought not to be dropped. It was well, they thought, that those who now opposed Mr. Napier's Bill should be reminded, in a practical way, that a more extreme demand lay behind it. Moreover, they considered that, in the temper of the then Government, it was within the range of possibility that Mr. Crawford's Bill might be accepted. They were determined that it should, at all events, be discussed. It was, therefore, decided that the measure should be again brought forward, and it was accordingly reintroduced by Mr. Justice Shee on the 25th November.

From him we learn what the Irish Parliamentary party thought about the Napier code, or rather about the "Tenants' Compensation Bill," which was the only part of the code in which they felt interested. The same judicial authority records for us the fate of the code.

"It is impossible," says Mr. Justice Shee, "to advert to the conduct of Mr. Napier, in relation to this question, and not acknowledge, that with the exception of Mr. Sharman Crawford, he did more

during the autumnal Session of 1852, and up to a
certain point, in Parliament, to advance the cause
of Irish Land Reform, than has been done by any
man living. Had it not been for the complexity
of the machinery of this Bill, and the illusory
nature in the case of inexhaustible improvements
of the compensation, partly by money payment,
and partly by what were called compensatory
periods of occupation provided by it, the code
would have been at once accepted as a satisfactory
settlement of the question. But debate arising
upon these defects, it was wisely resolved by Mr.
Disraeli, to refer all the Bills to a select committee,
and along with them, in respectful consideration to
the declared wishes of the Irish people, but without
affirmance (as malevolently to him suggested at
the time,) or even discussion of its principle and
details, Mr. Sharman Crawford's Bill."[7]

On the 20th December, the Government resigned,
and a Liberal administration, under the leadership
of Lord Aberdeen, succeeded to power.

In Feb., 1853, the select committee appointed
to consider the Napier Code, and Mr. Crawford's
Bill, met. Its members were : Lord Palmerston,

---

[7] " Papers, Letters, &c., on the Irish Land Question," by
Mr. Justice Shee, pp. 144, 150.

Mr. Shee had taken charge of the bill in consequence of
Mr. Crawford's absence, owing to illness.

the Home Secretary, Sir John Young, the Secretary for Ireland, Mr. J. D. Fitzgerald, Mr. Shee, Mr. Duffy, Mr. Lucas, Mr. Bright, Mr. James Sadlier, Mr. Walpole, Lord Naas, Mr. Napier, Mr. (afterwards Chief Justice) Whiteside, Mr. Dunlop, Dr. Phillimore, Colonel Greville, Mr. Pollard Urquhart, Mr. Roche, Lord Claude Hamilton, Mr. Davison, Mr. Grogan, Lord Monck, Mr. Kirk, and Mr. Vernon.

Mr. Shee relates briefly the result of the deliberations of the committee.

" Assenting to the provisions of the three first bills, which in the main were adopted by the committee, and afterwards by both Houses of Parliament, Lord Palmerston and Sir John Young voted for and procured the rejection upon its first clause of Mr. Crawford's Bill, and proposed, in the name of the cabinet, a modification of the " Tenants' Improvement Compensation Bill," by limiting the improvements for which compensation prospectively and retrospectively were to be claimed, to four classes.

1. The erecting or enlarging farm houses and farm buildings suitable to the holding, and adding to its letting value for agricultural purposes.
2. The reclamation of cut out bog and waste land, converting it into arable or pasture land.
3. The making of farm roads.

4. The making of boundary fences ;

" The compensation was to be by money payment, claimable only in case of eviction, or other
cause than non-payment of rent, or breach of
covenant ; and subject to every conceivable cross
demand, set-off, and deduction for arrears of rent,
rates, taxes, damages for breach of covenant, waste,
and dilapidation which a landlord, or any fair
valuer for him could claim." [*]

The Government now resolved to support as
amended all the four (Napier) bills. It was resolved
that all should be taken up as soon as possible to the
House of Lords ; and in the hope of a final adjustment before the session should close, day sittings
were appointed to expedite them.

The bills were read a third time in the Commons,
and sent up to the Lords in August.

It is due to Mr. Napier to state, that though now
in opposition, he did everything in his power to
facilitate the progress of the bills. Not so his
party. They offered an uncompromising opposition to the Tenants' bill. Taking advantage of
the fact that this measure had been amended in
committee (the amendments were rather of detail
than principle), Lord Derby considered that he
was no longer bound officially to support the
measure, and consequently went to the other ex-

[*] Ibid., p. 151.

H

treme, and backed up the landlords in their attack upon it. I shall again quote from Mr. Justice Shee as to what took place.

"Lord Derby not being '*officially bound*' to support the amended 'Tenants' Improvements Compensation Bill,' thought proper, through his friends, to oppose it ; at the wane of the London season, a flight of Irish landlords, bent on battle for their version of *quidquid solo plantatur solo cedit*, appeared at Westminster ; Lord Aberdeen was induced to defer legislation upon the question until the session of 1854; and before it opened, Mr. Napier, who from the time he explained the new Code to the House of Commons, had been exposed to a storm of obloquy from the organs of his party in Ireland, had again become conformable and ready to obey its behests." [1]

Despite the unpromising reception of the Code much progress had, nevertheless, been made with the land question. Mr. (now) Sir Charles Gavan Duffy, speaking in September, 1853, as to the result of the session's work, said, "I have reserved for the last the chief success of the Independent party —their success on the land question.

"I have declared elsewhere my belief that neither

[1] "Papers, Letters, &c., on the Irish Land Question," by Mr. Justice Shee, p. 150. The Irish landlords were led in the attack by Lord Clanricarde.

Catholic emancipation, reform, nor free trade, was ever pushed so far in a single session. We got the House of Commons to adopt and affirm, by considerable majorities, principles to which we were assured beforehand that they would not so much as listen. We got them to pass a bill which, whatever might be its shortcomings, had merits enough to be accepted by Mr. Sharman Crawford, the guardian of the question, and Mr. Serjeant Shee, to whom he has bequeathed his parliamentary position. I shall tell you, in a very cursory way, some of the provisions of the reformed land code. You know, all of you, that whatever improvements were made upon the land in Ireland, whether houses, agricultural buildings, fences, roads, or the like, became the property of the landlord. The maxim of the law was 'that whatever attaches to the freehold becomes part of the freehold.' By this maxim the proprietors have confiscated all the improvements of the tenants of Ireland for the last 200 years. A man was liable to severe penalties for injuring the very work he himself had made. Now, we have got the House of Commons to declare the directly opposite principle—that improvements are the property of the improver, that they are the property of the man who made them, and that he shall be entitled to sell, remove, or destroy them at his pleasure. This was blotting out at a stroke

the diabolical principle which had robbed and impoverished the farmers of Ireland, generation after
generation. But this was only protection for the
future. The immense sums which the tenants of
this fine county, and of almost every county in
Ireland, had spent on their farms, were still at the
mercy of the landlords. Here was our greatest
victory. We got the House of Commons to provide that whosoever could prove that he had
created permanent improvements on his farm, or
that those whom he succeeded, or from whom he
inherited at any distance of time had made them,
was entitled to recover their value from the landlord in case of eviction. At first it was proposed
to limit the amount he could recover to four years'
annual value of the farm, and to limit the time he
could go back in establishing his improvements to
twenty years, but both these limitations were
finally struck out, and a man was declared entitled
to the value of his existing improvements, whatever
they might actually be, and no matter at how distant a period they were created. In all former
Land Bills, from whatever party they sprang, the
tenant was required to furnish plans and specifica-
tions for future improvements, but this burthen-
some and impossible machinery was swept out of
the present Bill." [2]

[2] This speech was addressed to the electors of New Ross,

At the commencement of the session of 1854 the Bills of the Code were referred to a Select Committee of the House of Lords, and the result, briefly stated, was that the "Tenants' Compensation Bill" was condemned, and the other Bills sent down to the House of Commons without it.

So terminated the effort made by Mr. Napier to settle the Land Question.

On the 24th January, 1855, Lord John Russell retired from the ministry on the defeat of the Government on Mr. Roebuck's motion with reference to the conduct of the Crimean War. Soon afterwards Lord Aberdeen resigned, whereupon the Liberal Cabinet was reconstructed by Lord Palmerston, who became Prime Minister.

On the 20th February, 1855, Mr. Serjeant Shee asked for leave to bring in what was practically the rejected "Tenants' Compensation Bill" of the Napier Code. The Government accepted the principles of the bill "prospective" and "retrospective," but proposed as an amendment that the retrospective clauses should be limited to twenty years. This amendment was opposed by Mr. Serjeant Shee and the Irish party, but carried by the Government.

for which borough Sir Charles Gavan Duffy then sat. *Vide* Supplement of the *Freeman's Journal*, of September 29, 1853.

The Government now took charge of the measure, which was opposed, despite the limitation as to its retrospective operation, by the landlords.

As the measure stood it gave satisfaction to no one. The landlords opposed it as they opposed every attempt at legislation designed for the benefit of the tenants, and the tenant-right party opposed it as inferior to the Napier Code, and utterly inadequate to meet the needs of the case. Under such circumstances Lord Palmerston deemed it judicious to abandon the bill, and abandoned it accordingly was.

It was now resolved by the tenant-right party to bring forward Mr. Sharman Crawford's "Tenant-Right Bill," the object of which was, it will be remembered, the legalizing and extending of the Ulster Custom.[3] Mr. George Henry Moore was appointed leader of the party, and on the 19th Feb. 1856, he introduced the measure. It was read a second time on the 4th June without debate, but on the following day when Mr. Horsman, Irish Secretary, was interrogated by Mr. Stafford, an Irishman but an English member, as to the intentions of the Government with respect to the bill, he replied that they would oppose it. In the face of such an intimation, which came by surprise

[3] *Vide* ante, p. 77.

on the Irish party after the quiescent proceedings of the Government on the previous day, it was deemed useless to attempt further progress with the Bill that session. It was therefore dropped. On the 28th May, 1857, Mr. Moore brought the Bill forward again, but found it impossible to obtain a reasonably early day for its discussion before the end of the session, and so withdrew it.

Next year Mr. Maguire, as leader of the Irish party, reintroduced (on April 14th, 1858,) Mr. Serjeant Shee's "Tenants' Compensation Bill," in the hope that parliament might be more disposed to entertain it than the "Tenant-Right Bill," but the measure was defeated on the second reading by a majority of 200 to 65. Thus all efforts up to and including 1859 had failed to effect an amendment of the law of landlord and tenant in Ireland. " Meanwhile," says Mr. Finlason, " a settlement of the land question took place in India, based upon a ground quite in accordance with the principles of ancient law, and which went infinitely further than a mere right of compensation for improvements, viz., that a tenant, after a certain number of years, should be entitled to enjoy the land permanently at the same rent ; in other words, should have a perpetual inheritable tenancy." " It might have been well," continues the editor of *Reeves' History of English Law*, " if British statesmen had felt themselves able to propose for Ireland a measure similar to that which had thus been successfully carried in India, but it was not so, and when next year (1860) the Government proposed a measure to improve the tenure of land in Ireland, it was conceived that it was a mere measure of prospective compensation, accompanied with new leasing powers, and by a mere consolidation of the law.

" In 1860 an Act passed to amend the law relating to the tenure and improvement of land in Ireland,* which recited that it is expedient that provision should be made for facilitating improvements of landed property in Ireland, and which contained numerous provisions on the subject of the law of landlord and tenant.   It authorized limited owners to claim compensation for improvements made with judicial sanction.

" That part of the Act, as to tenants' improvements, which applied only to land let for *agricultural* purposes, provided that any tenant may, ' upon compliance with certain conditions,' one of which was the *landlord's consent*, make improvements, and may then, upon compliance with the conditions, be entitled to compensation for his outlay by way of annuity ; provided that the improve-

* 23 and 24 Vic. c. 153.

ments are not such as he is compellable to make by contract or custom.

"The nature of the improvements which the tenant was thus allowed—only upon compliance with the conditions imposed—was strictly defined. The conditions imposed were most stringent ; there was every possible limitation ; and lastly, there was no provision for retrospective compensation for past improvements.

"Under this Act leasing powers were given to 'limited owners' either to grant agricultural improvement leases, or building or repairing leases, upon certain terms prescribed in the Act—terms similar to those in the English Leasing Power Act. Agricultural leases, however, not to be for a longer term than *twenty-one years*, although it had long before been established that in cases of improvement they ought to be for sixty or one hundred years.

"This Act, it will be seen, did little to give the tenant protection, either by way of security for compensation or certainty of tenure. And it was accompanied by another, which, although apparently only a measure for consolidation, contained a provision calculated to deprive the tenant of any protection which the common law or custom might afford him.

"In the course of the long examination and discussion which the question had undergone, it had probably not escaped the minds of some lawyers that by the common law of England, which had been formally extended to Ireland, the tenant, by reason of the tenure between him and his landlord, was entitled to compensation for all improvements honestly made, and it was remembered that the Devon Commission had so reported many years before, and that the claims arising on that ground would now be formidable.   Perhaps it was on this account the Act contained the otherwise inexplicable enactment that the relation of landlord and tenant should thenceforth rest only on contract, and not on tenure.

" The object and the intended effect of this Act was to substitute, in the relation of landlord and tenant, for the just and equitable principles of common law or custom the hard commercial principle of contract, and to render any right of the tenant, either as to duration of tenancy or compensation, dependent on expressed or implied contract." [5]

Mr. Finlason touches upon important ground here.   There is no delusion more necessary to be dispelled from the English mind than that produced by the " contract " argument of the Irish landlord.   The Englishman who merely regards

[5] Finlason's " Land Tenure," pp. 120, 126.

the relation of landlord and tenant in Ireland from
the commercial contract point of view will never
succeed in comprehending the Irish land question.
Yet this is the point from which the English
public and the English Parliament are constantly
urged to consider and judge it.

Why do the tenants take the land, and offer
to pay the rent if they are not sure they can fulfil
their contracts, and why should the State have to
interfere in their bargains ? These are questions I
have heard asked over and over again. To the first
question the simple answer is, they cannot help
themselves in what they do. No Irish tenants
take land, believing beforehand that they cannot
pay, and intending not to pay. They of course
see difficulty and danger and hardship, and
struggle ahead ; but there is a merciless necessity
behind them. They make the best terms they
can, which, in truth, means bowing to whatever
the omnipotent master of the situation imposes.
They have practically no choice.

To the second question I shall reply in Irish
fashion, by asking another, Why does Parliament
regulate or fix and limit the price which a railway
company charges me for my travelling ticket ?
Why are not we, the " contracting " parties, the
railway company and myself, left to settle between
us how much the price in every particular case

shall be? It is because the law says we are not free contracting parties: the railway company has a monopoly of that which is, in a sense, a necessity to me and others: and if, when I stood at the ticket office, the matter were left to "contract," I should practically have to give them five shillings a mile if they demanded it.

In a country like Ireland a land monopoly is just as fatal to "free contract" between landlord and tenant. Where myriad trade industries so compete with land that its occupation is not absolutely a necessity of life, the case is not the same ; just as in places where there are half a dozen railways in the same direction, it is not the parliamentary prohibition, but their competition that regulates the fare.

In Ireland, as has often been truly said, "land is life." But apart from the one simple all-sufficient explanation of *monopoly*, there is a concurrent fact which is, perhaps, the most important of all. The tenant, as a rule, has, with his forefathers, occupied and tilled and improved the land from time immemorial. All the labour, all the savings of himself and his forefathers have been sunk in the plot of ground. He is unfitted for any other occupation. There are no other homesteads to choose from. Here is something worse than any monopoly which Parliament ever curbed.[6] Here is this tenant utterly at the landlord's mercy. Free contract is out of the question. In fact in that sense it is not contract at all.

I have said that if the pressure on the land was eased by the competition of trade industries, some elements of " free contract " might, no doubt, prevail. If I am asked why Ireland has not got those industries, although the question is purely collateral to the subject in hand, I have explanation in abundance.

[6] " In Ireland the landlord has a monopoly of the means of existence, and has a power for enforcing his bargains, which does not exist elsewhere—the power of starvation." (Lord Normanby in the House of Lords, Feb. 17, 1844.)

" However ignorant many of us may be of the state of Ireland, we have here (in the Devon Commission) the best evidence that can be procured—the evidence of persons best acquainted with that country, of magistrates of many years' standing, of farmers, of those who have been employed by the Crown ; and all tell you that the possession of land is that which makes the difference between existing and starving amongst the peasantry, and that therefore ejections out of their holdings are the cause of violence and crime in Ireland. In fact, it is no other than the cause which the great master of human nature describes when he makes a tempter suggest it as a reason to violate the law : ' Famine is in thy cheeks, need and oppression starveth in thine eyes, upon thy back hangs ragged misery. The world is not thy friend, nor the world's law; the world affords no law to make thee rich. Then be not poor, but break it.' " (Lord John Russell, Hansard, 3rd series, vol. lxxxvii. p. 507.)

The trade and commerce of the country was destroyed years ago by England.

"The English," says Mr. Froude, "deliberately determined to keep Ireland poor and miserable, as the readiest means to prevent it being troublesome. They destroyed Irish trade and shipping by navigation laws. They extinguished Irish manufactures by differential duties. They laid disabilities even on its wretched agriculture, for fear that Irish importations might injure the English farmer."[7]   With the destruction of the trade and commerce of the country the people were driven to the land—in the cultivation of which even they did not receive fair play—as their sole means of existence.

An order of landlords was created, between whom and their tenants there was not a single bond of sympathy. The landlords thought only of the rent, and they demanded the very highest. Their relations with their tenants were founded upon and regulated by commercial principles, though not possessing those incidents of commercial transactions which are calculated to place the contracting parties upon something like a

[7] "Romanism and the Irish Race," *North American Review*, January, 1880, p. 35. *Vide* also Mr. Lecky's reply to Mr. Froude's "English in Ireland in the Eighteenth Century," *Macmillan's Magazine*, January, 1873, p. 258. Appendix C.

footing of equality. Whilst demanding from the tenant an exorbitant rent, the landlord never seems to have considered whether the tenant would be able to pay it or not ; and, with greater culpability still, he opposed all reforms of the laws intended for improving the condition and promoting the prosperity and paying capabilities of the tenant.

The result of the vicious system of land tenure, for the maintenance of which the landlords are mainly responsible, has been the imperfect cultivation of the land, the impoverishment of the tenants, and the now threatened destruction of landlordism itself.

The landlords, to speak plainly and honestly, are chiefly to blame for the condition of things which has arisen. I do not mean to say that the landlords of to-day, or yesterday, or the day before, are to blame. It may be that, in some instances, they are the victims of the unwisdom of their ancestors. The latter, perhaps, have sown the wind, and the former are now reaping the whirlwind. At the same time, I cannot help observing that the present generation of landlords have done not a little to perpetuate the mischief.

But I shall be asked, why persist in recalling past memories ? Deal with the present state of things, it will be said, and say nothing about by-gone days.

"What did you eat yesterday, and how have you been in the habit of living generally?" says the doctor to the dyspeptic patient. "Oh, never mind yesterday," replies the patient. "My stomach is out of order now; just deal with *that*, and never mind the past." But the treatment of that patient, unless by a quack, must be based on well studied knowledge of the past. It is so with the Irish land question. The inquiry as to whether a man's great-grandfather had the gout is not less pertinent in treating a patient for a stinging pain in his big toe, than is the question as to what was the condition of the Irish tenant two centuries ago in dealing with the subject of Irish land-tenure to-day. The past has produced the present. The patient must be treated "historically."

Moreover, Irish tenants are sometimes spoken of in English society, by Irish landlords, as dirty, lazy, and almost uncivilized, without any reference whatever being made to the unfortunate circumstances in which they have been placed. Those tenants often can only be vindicated by a reference to the past. If the Irish tenants are not as far advanced as they might be, the landlords, the authors and supporters of the demoralizing laws under which they have been forced to live, are in a great degree responsible.[8] But the Irish tenants, in

---

[8] Lord Dufferin said, in 1854, "The present relation of

spite of generations of landlord legislation and misrule, are to-day intelligent, industrious, honest, and hard-working.

"The tenantry of Ireland," said Lord Palmerston, "when they receive encouragement, and have reason to believe that their exertions will meet with a due reward, are as much inclined to industrious exertion as the tenantry of any part of the world."[*]

The Act of 1860, happily, was in a large measure abortive. Had it succeeded, it would have done much more harm than good. "If the Act of 1860," says Mr. Finlason, "had been *successful*, it would have destroyed any claim of the tenant even to compensation for *future* improvements, unless in accordance with some *contract*, express or implied ; and, although a usage might be *evidence* of an implied contract, still it would have been necessary to prove contract. And as to the past, as already stated, it contained no provision whatsoever. Neither did it contain any provisions calculated to promote security of tenure, or right to compensation."

landlord and tenant in Ireland is of a barbarous character." Feb. 28, 1854.

[*] Hansard, May 4, 1855, p. 168. Between 1848 and 1864 the Irish emigrants had sent back to Ireland upwards of 13,000,000*l.* Lord Dufferin's "Irish Emigration, and Tenure of Land in Ireland," p. 3.

I

"On the contrary, as already seen, it contained a clause calculated to destroy the tenant's right to compensation, either as to the present or the past. The act, however, proved nugatory."[1] In fact, this Act of 1860 was a retrogression. The principle of retrospective improvements, established by the Napier code, was abandoned by it. The land question in truth had moved backward, from 1852 to 1845, instead of forward, from 1852 to 1860. The landlords were having it all their own way. "The question is," said Mr. Bright, in 1852, "can the cats legislate well and judiciously for the mice?" The question was answered in 1860. They could not.

A tide of emigration now set in. The people rushed from the land in thousands. Hope for them there had fled.

"You cannot evict a whole nation," Mr. John Stuart Mill once said with reference to Ireland; "the country would be made too hot to hold you, if you attempted it." But "a whole nation" was now passing away. The *Times*, in an article on the Irish exodus on the 3rd May, 1860, said, "Irish emigration still continues at a rate far beyond the calculations of the economist, and perhaps even the wishes of the statesman. If this goes on, and it is likely to go on, Ireland

[1] Finlason's " Land Tenure," p. 126.

will become very English, and the United States very Irish."

The *Times* did not seem to regret the first anticipated result of the Irish exodus very much. Its displeasure was apparently rather reserved for the last-mentioned contingency. To get the Irish out of Ireland, was a matter more to be promoted than retarded, provided no unpleasant after-results were likely to be produced. But here the *Times* had its forebodings and doubts. "We shall," said the great journal, sorrowfully, "only have pushed the Celt westwards." The *Times* feared that this westward movement of the Celt might have an unpleasant reactionary effect. The Irish were going with a vengeance, but it was possible they might come back with a vengeance too, or be the enemies of England in other lands. "We must," said the *Times*, "gird our loins to encounter the Nemesis of seven centuries of misgovernment. To the end of time 100,000,000 of people, spread over the largest habitable area in the world, and confronting us everywhere, by sea and land, will remember that their forefathers paid tithes to the Protestant clergy, rent to absentee landlords, and a forced obedience to the laws which these had made."

The Irish had, undoubtedly, gone with a vengeance. They were destined to come back with a vengeance. The exodus and clearances had sown "dragons' teeth from the Hudson to the Mississippi," and Fenianism had sprung up. This formidable conspiracy was hatched in America, between 1860 and 1865. In the latter year Ireland was in a state of rebellion. In 1866 another attempt was made to settle the land question. On the 30th April of that year Mr. Chichester Fortescue (now Lord Carlingford), brought in a bill to amend the Act of 1860. The effect of that Act, he said, was that the tenant, before improving, had to ask the landlord's consent; and this he described as "an invitation to the landlord to dissent." He now proposed that, in the absence of any written contract to the contrary, the tenant should, by the general rule of law, have a *limited* beneficial interest in the permanent improvement executed at his own cost. This bill pleased nobody. The tenants objected to the limitation, and fairly argued that if, as Mr. Fortescue said with reference to the bill of 1860, an attempt to get the landlord's consent was but "an invitation to him to dissent," so, under this measure, a provision enabling the landlord to forbid improvements by written contracts would be but an "invitation" to such a prohibition. The landlords, on the other hand, objected to the bill, as they objected to every measure of reform on the subject, no matter how inadequate and incomplete from the tenant's point of view. The bill fell through.

On the 18th February, 1867, another bill was brought in, this time by the Tories, who had, in the interval, succeeded to power. By this bill it was proposed that, instead of obtaining the landlord's consent before making improvements, the tenants should obtain the consent of a "commissioner of improvements." This was simply going back again to Lord Stanley's bill of 1845. Parliament was legislating, or rather attempting to legislate, in a circle. The tenants would have accepted Lord Stanley's bill in 1845. They would not accept it now. The lesson of the Sibylline books has never, I fear, been taken to heart by legislators.

The landlords objected to the bill also. They were, in fact, as stolid in their opposition to all legislative measures, intended to ameliorate the condition of the occupiers of the soil, as if Ireland was a land flowing with milk and honey, and the people in a state of perfect contentment.

The bill of 1867 was thus generally disapproved of, and finally abandoned.

Twenty-eight years had now gone by since the report of the Devon Commission was written, but its recommendations remained still neglected. No

legislative enactment had yet been passed to secure
to the tenant the property which his industry had
created in the soil.

The report of the Devon Commission had shared
the fate of all such reports. It had produced no
practical legislative results. A Parliament of landlords had legislated for landlords, and for landlords
alone. Nothing was accomplished for the tenants.
The cats could not be induced to legislate judiciously for the mice.

Such was the state of affairs on the dissolu-
tion of Parliament, on the 10th December,
1868.

The Liberal Party then went to the country with
"an Irish cry." The time had come, the leader of
that party thought, when something should be done,
and done with effect, to remove the evils which
affected Ireland, and brought discredit to the
Empire. There had been enough, and more than
enough, of Coercion Bills and Select Committees.
The day for practical legislation on a statesmanlike scale had arrived, and Mr. Gladstone determined to deal with, and settle, once for all, the
three great Irish questions then to the front—the
Church, Education, and, above all, the Land.

The events of the past few years in Ireland had
attracted the attention of the English public in a
special manner.

It was abundantly clear to thoughtful men that Irish loyalty could only be gained by the redressing of Irish wrongs ; and that whilst the Irish Protestant Church continued to exist as a State establishment, and the law of landlord and tenant remained unaltered, disaffection would prevail. Mr. Gladstone now resolved that the one should cease to exist, and that the other should be reformed.

The General Election resulted in the accession of a Liberal Ministry, under the leadership of Mr. Gladstone, to power ; on the 26th July, 1869, the Irish Protestant Church, as a State establishment, practically ceased to exist. On the 15th February, 1870, Mr. Gladstone brought in a bill to amend the law of landlord and tenant in Ireland. It was read a second time on the 14th March, by a majority of 442 to 11.[2] And having passed through the Lords with some alterations, of a more or less important nature, received the royal assent on the 1st August, 1870. Something had, at last, been done to carry out the recommendations of the Devon Commission.

I have said that Mr. Napier's bill, of 1853, was a

[2] The eleven were chiefly composed of Irish members, led by Sir John Gray, who thought, that, the bill did not go far enough, and would fail, because sufficient means were not provided by it for giving the tenant that security which, beyond all doubt, it was the object of Mr. Gladstone to establish.

great step in advance.   But Mr. Napier was forced
to retreat.   " Every leading statesman," said Mr.
Napier, when justifying himself in 1853 to Lord
Donoughmore, " including the late Lord George
Bentinck, the House of Lords, and every section of
the House of Commons, has given an avowed sanc-
tion to the principle of a Tenant Compensation
Bill for Ireland." [3]

But in 1855 Mr. Napier was compelled to write
in different tones.   " It is notorious," he then said,
" that the House of Lords will pass no such
measure, and that for a Government to propose it
to them, or pretend to support it, is an imposture
and a sham." [4]

Mr. Gladstone now made a great stride in advance, and he held his ground.   The wreckage of
previous measures was swept away.   Mr. Gladstone
did not attempt, as all the statesmen since 1845
had attempted, to construct a scheme out of the
timbers of old plans.   He built anew with fresh
materials all his own.

The consent of the landlord, or of a " Commissioner of Improvements," was no longer made essential to entitle the tenant to recover compensation on
eviction for the property added by him without

[3] " Letters and Papers, &c., on the Irish Land Question,"
by Mr. Justice Shee, p. 154.
[4] Ibid., 155.

the knowledge of either to the soil. The attempt which in the past had sometimes been made by Ulster landlords to defeat the Ulster Custom, were rendered impossible in the future, for that custom now received the sanction of law. The question of "prospective" and "retrospective" improvements was, for ever, set at rest. It was a last declared by Parliament that the tenant should, whether the landlord willed it or not, reap the fruits, existing, or to come, of his labour and industry.*

Mr. Gladstone's Land Act, however, has not, as we all know, been accepted as a final settlement of the land question. Nor do I think that any of the statesmen who were chiefly concerned in its introduction, or passage through Parliament, thought it would be so accepted at the time. It was a step, and the greatest made since the Union, towards a final settlement, that was all ; not but that was much. Until Mr. Gladstone's time, Parliament had altogether legislated in the interests of the landlords. The common law of the country had been amended to give them additional powers over the properties of their tenants.[5] Ejectments had been made "cheap and easy," and the result was that 'notices to quit fell like snowflakes" on the people. Mr. Gladstone tried to make ejectments "dear and difficult," but, unhappily

* *Vide* Note, p. 222.   [5] *Vide* Appendix D.

the notices to quit fall like "snowflakes" still.

The defect in the Land Act would seem to be, that it did not, in express terms, place the tenant absolutely beyond the capricious control of the landlord.

The Act was curative, rather than preventive. It left the landlord in possession of all the old powers, which he had often abused, but at the same time provided means, not previously in existence, of fining him when he did wrong. He might rack rent, and evict as much as ever, but he could no longer, by *law*, confiscate the property of his tenant as he had formerly done. Before the Land Act, if a tenant possessed bog land at the rent of 10*s.* an acre, and if, by his industry, he had made it worth 4*l.* an acre, the landlord could, and frequently did, increase the rent. This increase, as Mr. Gladstone said, when introducing his Land Act, being " founded upon the value which the capital and labour of the tenant had added to the soil." [6] Assuming that the tenant was unable to pay the increased rent, he was evicted, without receiving one shilling's worth of compensation for the improvements which had been made by him. Now, what the Land Act has done, is this: it has still left the landlord power to raise the rent capri-

[6] Hansard, 3rd series, vol. cxcix. p. 347.

ciously in proportion as the value of the land is increased by the " labour and capital" of the tenant. Thus the tenant is practically obliged to pay a yearly mulct because of his industry and outlay. It is only in case of eviction that the land Act entitles him to be reimbursed. Of course, hating eviction, and clinging to the land as all Irish tenants do, the bulk of them submit to this legalized plunder, rather than seek the protection of the Land Act at the price of eviction.

The landlords, however, have not been prevented from unfair rent-raising and unjustly evicting, on account of the penalties, which, by way of compensation, they might be compelled to pay, for so doing.

Those penalties have fallen too lightly upon them, and they have been enabled to recoup themselves, by the increased rent, for the sums which they have been obliged to pay to evicted tenants as compensation for improvements.

On the other hand, the tenants have not, in the majority of cases, been at all adequately recompensed for the loss of their holdings by the sums which they have received.

The procedure which they have been obliged to adopt is litigious, expensive to them, and well calculated, upon the whole, to defeat the policy of the Act. They have, in the first instance, to sue the

landlord before the County Court Judge. Then, if
he appeals, they are compelled to go before the
Judge of Assize; and thus a good deal of expense
is incurred by the tenant, in law costs, before he
receives any compensation at all. When, finally,
he does receive a sum as compensation, it often turns
out to be wholly insufficient as a remedy for the
loss of his farm, and for the trouble and expense
he has been put to.

A case occurred in the County Cork, only a
few months ago, which will illustrate what I
mean. I shall state the facts in the words of
Mr. Justice Lawson, before whom the case was
tried :—

"The facts," said Judge Lawson, "are undisputed. A great many years ago this man (the
tenant) became the yearly tenant of this little
mountain tract or bog, containing eighteen acres,
or thereabouts, at the small yearly rent of 7*l.* 15*s.*,
but quite enough, considering what the condition
of the farm then was. It appears that this man,
with that industry which characterizes very often
people in his position, set at once about cultivating
and reclaiming that piece of land, spreading lime
on it, and gradually reducing it to a better state
than before. He so continued as tenant from year
to year until 1869, and in that year the present
appellant, Edmund Murphy, having purchased up

the interest in the land over him, became the
intermediate landlord of Mahony, and induced him
to take a lease for ten years at the rent of 18*l.* a
year—a most enormous rent—for, according to all
the facts before me, I don't think that at any
period during his occupancy the real letting value
of this farm was more than 14*l.* or 15*l.* in its best
state. Well, the man struggled, as he paid his
18*l.* a year for ten years, and at the end of that
time the landlord, in the undoubted exercise of his
right, put him out. But if the landlord had an
undoubted right to put him out, it was equally his
undoubted right to give the tenant whatever compensation would be fairly awarded to him under
the Land Act. The tenant having been put out
of possession, he makes his claim under the 4th
section of the Act for buildings, reclamation, fences,
and unexhausted manures, and the chairman
allowed him a certain sum of money, which, with
rent and costs deducted, made the total amount
of the decree 66*l.* 8*s.* 1*d.*—a sum, I am bound to
say, quite inadequate to compensate this old man
for having been turned out of his holding, on
which he lived and laboured for so many years."
" The landlord," added the learned judge, " has
received for the last ten years a rent considerably
more than the letting value of it. He chooses to
put this man out, and to take possession now into

his own hands, and he refused to be bound by a most honest and considerate award, made by a deceased clergyman, who, I have no doubt, did everything that was right in the case. He refused in the most obstinate manner to allow this old man to remain in possession himself, and the reason of that was because Mahony's land got into the middle of the farm, because the surrounding tenants were all evicted, and the work of eviction was completed by the landlord ejecting this man. The law allows him to do that, but he must pay for it, and the sum the chairman has given I will not reduce by one single penny. The chairman is a better judge of those manures and reclamations than I am; but I am bound to say that if the chairman had given a considerably larger sum than 75*l.* I would be quite prepared to adopt it." [7]

The question now is, can the Land Act be so amended as to give the tenant real security of tenure? No scheme for the settlement of the " Irish Difficulty " which does not directly secure this end will, to my mind, be ever accepted as final. The Irish tenants—the Irish people—must be rooted in the soil; until this is done there will be no contentment, no peace in Ireland. All the just rights of the landlords

[7] *Freeman's Journal*, July 26, 1880.

must be preserved inviolate. But "rights" that are not just, or which are exercised unjustly, must be taken away. The power of arbitrary eviction is not just, and its exercise in the future must be made impossible. Let every care be taken, by all means, to guard "the sacredness of property;" but like anxiety must be evinced to protect what Daniel O'Connell used to call the "sacredness of possession." The Irish tenant believes as confidently in the justice of the latter as the Irish landlord does in the justice of the former. He thinks that the man who cultivates the land has an indisputable right to the possession. He feels that the tenant is entitled to deal with the "possession" as the landlord would be entitled to deal with the "property." He considers that the tenant should not be disturbed from the possession so long as he pays a fair rent ; i.e. a rent not to be arbitrarily fixed and altered by the landlord at pleasure, but to be adjudged as reasonably representing the value of the possession by a competent authority, standing between himself and the landlord. He further maintains, that if the landlord should insist on disturbing the tenant for any cause whatever, then that the latter has the right to dispose of the possession as best he can, without any interference on the part of the former.

I do not think it will serve any practical purpose

to consider or discuss whether those views of the Irish tenantry are theoretically correct or not. They may be right, or they may be wrong. The English land system may be the best system in the world, as some people think, or the very worst, as others aver. The Irish notions of land tenure may be undeserving of toleration, or they may be infinitely superior and more advantageous in every way to the community than the English. The question, at the best, is an open one. It is just as likely that the Irish are right as that the English are right. It was the opinion of John Stuart Mill that the Irish were right.

" The Irish circumstances and the Irish ideas as to social and agricultural economy," says Mr. Mill, " are the general ideas and circumstances of the human race. It is the English ideas and circumstances that are peculiar. Ireland is in the main stream of human existence, and human feeling and opinion. It is England that is in one of the lateral channels."[8]

But whether the Irish views are right, or whether they are wrong, the fact of their existence must be recognized and dealt with. The Irish peasantry have held those views for three hundred years. All that drastic legislation could do has been done to eradicate them, but in vain. For three hundred

[8] Hansard, May 17, 1866.

years the English Government have stood by and championed the landlords, and what has been the result? The estrangement and disaffection of a people whose "foible," to use the language of Swift, "is loyalty."

Either of two things must now be done. The old policy of doing everything for the landlord and nothing for the tenant—everything for the "English garrison" and nothing for the Irish people—must be resumed and carried out to the bitter end; or the new policy initiated in 1868 of governing Ireland according to "Irish ideas" must be firmly adhered to. If the first is to be the policy of the future, then it may be expected that the history of the past will repeat itself. Ireland will remain dissatisfied, and must continue to be ruled, not as an integral part of the empire, like Scotland, but as a subjugated and distrusted nation, like India. A standing army must still be maintained to preserve order in the country.[9] The old *régime* of Coercion Acts, military law, and the suspension of Constitutional Government in the island, must be revived and perpetuated. But if, on the other hand, the policy of 1868 in its full and legitimate development is to

---

[9] The strength of the Royal Irish constabulary alone—as perfect a military force as any England can send into the field—is nearly 12,000 men.

K

be the policy of the future, then an era of prosperity and peace, hitherto unknown, will at last dawn upon the land. The "shadow of the curse of past wrongs" will disappear when the substance of bad government is gone, and there shall be no longer "afflicting memories that cannot sleep," when the policy that arouses them has been for ever abandoned.

But how are these results to be brought about by constitutional and practical legislation ? How are the "sacred rights" of possession to be acknowledged consistently with preserving inviolate the "sacred rights" of property ? It can be done. It has in a large degree been already done in Ireland. In Ulster the "sacred rights" of possession are acknowledged, and the "sacred rights" of property remain inviolate. Let us study this Ulster lesson.

VI.

THE ULSTER CUSTOM.

PART I.: ORIGIN.

NEARLY three centuries ago there was a land question in the North of Ireland, as there is a land question in the south to-day. The main features of the one resembled in many respects those of the other.

Dr. Brewer, in his introduction to the " Carew State Papers" (1603—1624), thus describes what the nature of land-tenure was in the north, as well as in other parts of Ireland, on the accession of James I.: "Regular tenure of land, vested rights, were unknown among them [the tenants], each man having no more than a 'scrambling transitory possession,' at the pleasure of the chief. The more careful and industrious the tenant, the more liable he was to oppressions of all kinds—the more likely to be turned out of his holding." " What chance (says Dr. Brewer), could there be for order or improvement? Who would build farmhouses or

K 2

granges, in the possession of which he could not be assured for a twelvemonth?"[1]

Thus, it will be seen that uncertainty of tenure was the evil to be remedied in Ulster in 1603. Uncertainty of tenure is the evil to be remedied in Munster, Leinster, and Connaught, in 1880. This uncertainty was regarded as the great hindrance to the pacification of Ireland in the seventeenth century. This is the great hindrance to the pacification of Ireland in the nineteenth.

It will, therefore, I think, be neither uninteresting, nor uninstructive, to consider what was the policy adopted by the statesmen of the time of James I. to remove the great Irish grievance which confronted them, and which still confronts their successors.

The Irish Land Question of the seventeenth century was a legacy bequeathed by the government of Elizabeth to the government of James. In her reign grants of land in Ireland had been made chiefly to English lords. The policy of Elizabeth was to plant an English landlord colony in Ireland, and to govern the country from that centre. Considerations for the "mere Irish" she

[1] "Introduction to Carew State Papers," 1603 — 1624, p. 14.

had none. They were either to be rooted out, or kept as hewers of wood and drawers of water to the "Saxon" lords in their native land.[2]

"There was no care taken," says Sir John Davis, referring to the Elizabethan settlement, "of the inferior septs of people. There was but one freeholder made in a whole country, which was the lord himself; all the rest were but tenants-at-will, who by reason of the uncertainty of their estates, did utterly neglect to build, or to plant, or to improve the land. And, therefore," concludes this great English authority, alluding to the results of the Elizabethan policy, "although the lords were to become the king's tenant, the country was no whit reformed thereby, but remained in the former barbarism and desolation."[3]

Immediately upon the accession of James it was resolved that an attempt should be made to reclaim Ireland from the state of "barbarism and desolation" in which it had been left by Elizabeth. For this purpose Sir John Davis and Sir Arthur Chichester were sent to the country, the former in 1603, the latter in 1604. Sir Arthur came as

---

[2] It was ordered by Elizabeth that none of the English to be planted in Ireland should make any estate to the mere Irish. *Vide* "State Papers," 1586—1588, p. 86.

[3] "The Discovery of the True Cause why Ireland was never Subdued," by Sir John Davis, Solicitor-General to James I. p. 271.

Viceroy, and Sir John Davis as what, in modern phraseology, we should probably call the Chief Secretary.

Arrived in Ireland, the Viceroy and his great colleague turned their attention, in the first instance, to the reformation of what they deemed "the most rude and unreformed" part of the country—the province of Ulster. There, as in Munster, the system of tenancies-at-will existed. This system Sir John Davis condemned, and determined to use his best endeavours to suppress. It had worked mischief in England, he thought, and would work mischief in Ireland too, if allowed to continue. Writing to Cecil, on the 19th April, 1604, he says: "Certainly such tenants-at-will enabled the Earl of Warwick, in the reign of Henry VI., and the great lords in the times of the barons' wars, to raise so great a multitude of men; whereas, at this day, if any of the great lords of England should have a mind to stand upon their guard, well may they have some of their household servants, or some few light-brained, factious gentlemen, to follow them. But as for their tenants, who have good leases for years, or, being but copyholders—seeing that by law at this day they may bring an action for trespass against their lords if they dispossess them without cause of forfeiture—those fellows will not hazard the losing of their sheep, and their corn, and the undoing of themselves, for the best landlord that is in England." Convinced, at this early period of his visit and inspection, that the best means for pacifying and reforming Ulster would be the establishment of a system of certainty of tenure, Sir John winds up his despatch by expressing a hope that in the next Parliament an Act would be passed enjoining "every great lord to make such certain durable estates to his tenants, which would be good for themselves, good for their tenants, and good for the commonwealth." [4]

By the wholesale confiscations which followed upon the flight of Tyrone, an unexpectedly favourable opportunity was afforded Chichester and Davis for commencing the work of "plantation." They availed themselves of it with promptitude and sagacity. In the first place the tenants of the fugitive earls were assured that they should not be evicted. A royal proclamation was issued, declaring that they "should not be disturbed in the peaceable possession of their lands, so long as they demeaned themselves dutiful subjects." [5]

The policy of Elizabeth in Munster had been a

---

[4] "Calendar of State Papers (Ireland)," 1603 — 1606, p. 160.

[5] "Calendar of State Papers (Ireland)," 1606 — 1608, p. 263.

policy of extermination. It was apparently not the intention of Chichester and Davis to pursue to the same extent a similar course in Ulster. The next step taken was the appointment of Sir Toby Caulfield as receiver over the lands of the exiled earls. The disposition to propitiate and reassure the tenants, shown in the royal proclamation, was exhibited in the instructions given to Sir Toby Caulfield for his guidance as receiver. He was directed " not to innovate in any manner of collecting or gathering rents ;" but, on the contrary, "to make it appear that the king would be a more gracious landlord than Tyrone was, or could be."[6]

Meanwhile, on the 17th September, 1607, Chichester wrote to the Privy Council, advising— in the same spirit of conciliation—that the lands of Tyrone and Tyrconnell should be "divided amongst [1] the inhabitants—to every man of note, or good desert, as much as he can conveniently stock by himself, and his tenants ; [2] to bestow the rest upon servitors and men of worth here, and [3] to bring in colonies of civil people in England and Scotland."[7]

This policy of conciliation was not, however, I

[6] "Calendar of State Papers (Ireland)," 1608 — 1610, p. 534.

[7] "Calendar of State Papers (Ireland)," 1606 — 1608, pp. 275-6.

think it may be inferred, regarded with favour by all parties in England. There were some to whom the adoption of more drastic remedies for the settlement of Ulster would have been preferable. There was an extermination party—an Elizabethan survival, so to say—in England. Chichester apparently knew this ; and, anxious to carry all parties along with him, or at least to show a desire to meet, so far as it was possible, the views of all, he suggested, as an alternative course, in the event of the first proposal not being accepted, that the old inhabitants might be driven from the *rich* lands of Tyrone and Tyrconnell, to the *waste* districts over the Blackwater and the Bann. He, however, took pains to express his own preference for the first and milder course." [8]

In less than a fortnight a reply came from the Privy Council endorsing the conciliatory policy of the Viceroy. " The king," says the Privy Council, " in general approves of Chichester's project, being resolved to make a mixture of the inhabitants, as well Irish as English and Scotch ; to respect and favour the Irish that are of good note and desert, and to make Chichester specially judge thereof. [9]

[8] " Calendar of State Papers (Ireland)," 1606 — 1608, p. 277.

[9] " Calendar of State Papers (Ireland)," 1606 — 1608, p. 290.

The Lord Deputy, finding the Privy Council in so favourable a mood for his purposes, pushed on vigorously with his scheme. On the 14th Oct., 1608, he gave to Sir John Davis a code of instructions with reference to the contemplated plantation. In these instructions Chichester deals separately with the counties where it was intended that the experiment should first be tried, varying the details of the scheme to meet the circumstances of each particular district.

But the main drift of the instructions was this: to conciliate the natives; to settle them in considerable proportions upon the lands; not to dispossess them unless where such a course was rendered absolutely necessary in order to secure the subjugation of the province; above all, to diminish the power of the landlords; to cut down the estates of the large owners; and to establish, at all points, an independent body of small freeholders.

Here we notice another fresh departure from the Elizabethan policy. In Munster Elizabeth had created an order of great landowners.[1] In Ulster it was the desire of Chichester to establish a class of small proprietors. The land, he says, ought to be "divided into parcels and disposed to several freeholders." . . . Care should be taken, he adds,

[1] Dr. Brewer's "Introduction to the Carew State Papers," 1603—1624, p. 31.

that "the greatest part of the people should have their dependency immediately upon the king, and as little upon the lords as may be, without apparent hindrance to the plantation settlement."

As to the dispossession of the natives, he says: " Many of the natives in each county claim freehold in the lands they possess ; and, albeit, their demands are not justifiable by law, yet it is hard, and almost impossible to displant them. Wishes, therefore, that consideration may be had of the best and chief of them." [2]

Possessed of these "instructions," Davis proceeded to England, bearing with him, at the same time, a letter from Chichester, which, with the instructions, he was directed by the Lord Deputy to lay before the Privy Council. The letter was little more than a repetition of the views expressed in the "instructions." In it, as in them, he urges upon the Council the advisability of settling the natives in the soil, and of breaking down the landlord system, creating a small resident proprietary instead. " The escheated lands," he says, " should not be granted away in gross, or by whole counties to any one man, but rather be divided amongst many, and in reasonable proportions. Yet in such a way as to encourage the particular settlers to lay

[2] " Calendar of State Papers (Ireland)," 1608 — 1610, pp. 54—63.

their fortunes upon the plantation and the improvement thereof. "Consideration," he adds, "must be had of the natives, who are many," that "envy may be quenched."[3]

The work, or rather the policy, of the plantation did not now continue to proceed as smoothly as hitherto. The opposition to Chichester's conciliatory plans increased. The party of extermination in England were making way. The Lord Deputy, however, was resolved to stand by his guns, and never lost an opportunity of defending and strengthening the positions he had taken up. Writing to the Earl of Northampton on the 5th February, 1609, he again alludes to the subject of settling the natives. "They must," he says, "be provided for, or removed. The latter may be spoken of, and wished for, but hardly, and not without great expense, attained."[4]

On the 9th March, 1609, Chichester received a reply from the Privy Council touching the question of plantation. It was proposed to alter his scheme in some important points, and a disposition less favourable to the claims and rights of the natives was shown.

[3] "Calendar of State Papers (Ireland)," 1608 — 1610, p. 68.
[4] "Calendar of State Papers (Ireland)," 1608 — 1610, pp. 145-6.

Chichester promptly replied to this communication. On the very next day (10th March, 1609,) he wrote to the Privy Council, criticizing their amendments, and suggesting fresh alterations. He thought a commission ought to be appointed to deal with the whole subject, and that considerable discretion should be given to the commissioner, both as to the question of allotments generally, and the extent to which provision should be made for the natives. " There are many more of these," he says, " claiming and in expectation of freeholds than seems to have been considered of . . . and," he adds, " the quantity of land [proposed to be allotted], and the number of freeholders [proposed to be made], has been thought very small." This disposition to " exclude the natives produced a great deal of discontent throughout the country." So much so that, Chichester was obliged to send out the judges on circuit earlier than usual, with instructions to declare that the king was " graciously pleased to settle every principal man in a competent freehold." [5]

On the 31st March, 1609, Chichester, who was indefatigable in his exertions, followed up this letter with another to Davis, warning the Privy Council against the adoption of a rigorous policy

[5] "Calendar of State Papers (Ireland)," 1608 — 1610, p. 157 *et seq.*

The "course of displanting" even the "swordsmen," he says, "must not be thought upon," unless,
indeed, "the king will be at the charge of an army
as great as any in the last rebellion," and he adds,
"what fire such an insurrection [likely to be caused
by expelling the swordsmen] may enkindle in other
parts of the kingdom we know not."[6]

However, to the *mere* removal of the swordsmen Chichester had no objection, provided they
could be induced *voluntarily* to depart. But
he was opposed to the use of force. He saw the
dangers of a policy of coercion. He was desirous of
trying what moral persuasion could effect, and he
ultimately prevailed upon the Government in England to share his views in this matter.

On the 9th of June, 1609, he received instructions, framed in a more conciliatory spirit, for the
removal of the "swordsmen." He was told to
"use all persuasion to induce them to remove to
the *waste* lands," or "to facilitate their enlistment
in foreign service, and to supply them with funds at
the king's expense."[7]

These instructions Chichester cautiously and
effectually carried out. Some of the swordsmen he

[6] "Calendar of State Papers (Ireland)," 1608 — 1610,
p. 177.

[7] "Calendar of State Papers (Ireland)," 1608 — 1610,
p. 238.

"induced" to settle upon the *waste* lands, where they, and their descendants, for many generations, continued to remain an industrious and hard-working tenantry, endeavouring "to force a churlish soil for scanty bread." Others "enlisted in foreign service," and in many an honourable battlefield attested the wisdom of Chichester in not attempting to drive them from their native land by force.

Fresh dangers now arose to try the skill and astuteness of Chichester. Some of the Elizabethan landlords of the south evinced a disposition to move northwards, and "plant" in Ulster. This threatened incursion of southern landlords Chichester did not like. Their "ways" in Munster had not, he knew, tended much to the pacification of that province, and he looked suspiciously upon their advent to the new colony. One of those lords, Lord Audley, applied to the king for a grant of 100,000 acres in Tyrone. His lordship detailed, in an elaborate and pretentious letter, his schemes for reclaiming the county, and "planting" it, on a scale of great magnificence. But Chichester had no faith in Lord Audley or his "schemes." The Lord Deputy seemed to think that his lordship would be no acquisition to the plantation, and that he might, with advantage to Ulster, at all events, be allowed, or constrained, to remain south of the

Boyne. " Lord Audley," says the Viceroy, with a refreshing touch of humour, " is an ancient noble-man, and apt to undertake much ; but the manner of his life in Munster, and the small cost he has bestowed to make his house fit for him, does not promise much for the building of substantial castles, nor a convenient plantation in Ulster."

Always mindful, as a matter of policy, of the natives, and knowing what little consideration they would receive from men like my Lord Audley, Chichester observes, alluding to the unfavourable conditions proposed respecting them in the con-templated grant to Audley, that " if the natives be not better provided for in the conditions of the grant than I have yet heard of, they will kindle many a fire in Lord Audley's buildings before they be half-finished." [8]

Chichester, however, failed to prevent altogether the invasion of landlords, alike from England and Scotland, as well as the south of Ireland. But he, probably, checked the tide of invasion, and by se-curing good terms for the tenants, who were to live under those lords, mitigated, in some degree, the evils which southern landlordism had produced. Lord Audley received his grant ; not, however, for " 100,000 acres," which, as Chichester observed,

[8] " Calendar of State Papers (Ireland)," 1608 — 1610, p. 297.

"were more than the whole county," but for 3000.

There was only one other great English lord who received a grant—Lord Say. But the Scots were more fortunate.

The following Scottish lords received grants :— Lord Ochiltre for 3000 acres in Tyrone ; the Earl of Abercorn for 3000 acres in the same county ; and the Duke of Lennox for 3000 acres, and Lord Minto for 1000, both in Donegal. The names of other Scotch noblemen are to be found in the favoured list, notably the House of Hamilton.[9]

Despatches continued now to pass frequently to and fro between Chichester and the Privy Council. Those of Chichester were marked by the same tone of politic conciliation, and the same spirit of judicious considerateness towards the natives, which had, hitherto, characterized his communications. But a disposition equally fair and wise, was not exhibited by the Government in England. The extermination party were getting the upper hand.

Nevertheless Chichester did not abate his efforts to counteract their influences, and to carry out, so far as it was then possible, his original scheme. One thing he was firmly resolved upon, viz. that the extermination party should not have it *all* their

[9] " Calendar of State Papers (Ireland)," 1603 — 1624, p. 232 *et seq.*

L

own way.   A compromise scheme might in the end become inevitable, but no system of wholesale clearances should ever be adopted in Ulster, with his sanction or connivance.

The " undertakers " from Scotland and England now began to arrive, and the business of allotment was being proceeded with.

In the regulation of these allotments faith was not kept with the natives.

Of this Chichester bitterly complained.   " The natives," he says in a letter to Salisbury on the 27th September, 1610, "are discontented, and repine at their fortunes, and the small quantities of land left to them, especially in Tyrone, Armagh, and Colerayne . . ."   " They had," he proceeds, " assured themselves of better conditions from the king, than from their former landlords, but now they say they have not land given them, nor can they be admitted as tenants, which is very grievous to them."   But what Chichester seemed to feel most sorely was, that *he* had been made the medium of holding out promises and hopes which were now to be broken, and disappointed.   " I could," he says, with the sensitiveness of a man of honour, " have prevailed with them in any reasonable matter, but now I am discredited amongst them." [1]

[1] " Calendar of State Papers (Ireland)," 1608 — 1610, p. 160.

The extermination party had been wise in their generation. They had refrained from completely declaring their cards until the swordsmen were gone, but now they began to show their hands.

Chichester, however, in the absence of the "swordsmen," endeavoured to pursue the same policy which he had initiated before their removal. His letter to Salisbury, from which I have quoted, was not written without effect.

The plantation scheme was further modified, and though the natives did not obtain such good terms as Chichester desired, and stoutly contended for, yet they were not entirely forgotten.

Contrasted with the treatment which their fellow-countrymen in the south had received under Elizabeth's "plantation" policy, the Irish of the north were favoured.

A "compromise" scheme was ultimately arrived at, based upon Chichester's proposal, that the settlement should consist of a mixture of Irish, English, and Scotch, but modified by the imported conditions, that the English and Scotch should have the "fat" lands and the Irish the "lean."

The total number of acres "settled" in the plantation counties—Tyrone, Armagh, Donegal, Fermanagh, Derry, and Cavan — consisted of 511,465. Of these 209,000 were granted to the

English and Scotch, and 110,330 to servitors and natives. Reservations were made for free schools to be erected in the several counties, for the clergy, and for corporate towns. Of the allotted lands, fifty Englishmen divided 81,500 acres, and fifty Scotchmen 81,000 respectively between them. No Scotchman, and no Englishman was allowed to hold more than 3000 acres as his share, and very few of either (in fact, but two Englishmen and five Scotchmen) availed themselves of the maximum limit. The average amount of acres held by each person was between 1000 and 2000. Here was a marked feature of distinction between the northern and southern "plantations." Elizabeth's grants in Munster were, as compared to James's grants in Ulster, gigantic. Thus we find that 10,000 acres were given by Elizabeth to Sir Christopher Hatton in Waterford, 12,000 to Sir Walter Raleigh, 13,000 to Sir W. Herbert in Kerry, 24,000 to Jane Beecher and Hugh Worth, 11,000 to Arthur Hyde, 10,000 to Sir William Courtney in Limerick, 11,000 to Sir G. Lytton in Tipperary, 11,000 to Sir G. Boucher, and so on.

The economic grants of James I were productive of results as beneficial to Ulster, as the extravagant grants of Elizabeth had been productive of results injurious to Munster.

The former were calculated to, and did lead to

absenteeism : the latter to the establishment of a resident proprietary. "The enormous estates," says Dr. Brewer, "in Munster induced men of large fortunes and high birth to purchase." But those men had "no intention and no inducements to reside on those Irish estates, where their presence would have been invaluable."

Affairs were differently contrived in Ulster. The larger proportion of the English and Scotch settlers there, were squires and gentry who were not unwilling to settle in Ireland, and to live upon, and personally superintend the cultivation and improvement of their lands. Those men either did not possess the will, or had not the facilities for moving in "London Society," and either disposed by temperament, or constrained by circumstances, they lived in their new country, and endeavoured, in some instances, to discharge the duties, as well as to enjoy the rights of property.

The Ulster landlords, who in time became absentees, degenerated from the original stock. The Munster landlords who became absentees were "chips off the old blocks."[2]

Having obtained the best terms *he* could for the "natives," and "settled" the landlord order in a

[2] *Vide* Dr. Brewer's "Introduction to the Carew Calendar of State Papers," 1603—1624, p. 32 *et seq.*, as to the southern and northern plantations.

manner most calculated for the effectual achievement of his plans, Chichester next devoted himself with equal solicitude to the consideration of the tenant classes. He knew that a contented tenantry was as essential to the success of his project as a contented landocracy. He was resolved that Ulster should have both. To this end, and in order that "there might be repose and establishment of every subject's estate—lord and tenant, freeholder and farmer—throughout the kingdom," "special care," Sir John Davis tells us, "was taken to settle and secure the under-tenants."[3]

On the 20th August, 1610, Chichester issued a proclamation, in which it was declared that every landlord should "covenant to make certain estates to the under-tenants, with reservations of certain rents."[4]

In the next year (April 13th, 1611), the Lord Deputy submitted to the Privy Council in England a series of "propositions" respecting the "plantation," and, amongst other things, he laid it down as a matter to be accepted, or at least considered, by the Government, that as long as the British landlords "receive their rents from the natives they should never remove them."[5]

[3] Sir John Davis's "Discovery," &c. p. 273.
[4] "Ca endar of State Papers (Ireland)," 1608 — 1610, p. 490.
[5] "Calendar of State Papers (Ireland)," 1611—1614, p. 35.

The result of Chichester's negotiations was, that the Government caused to be inserted in every grant given to the landlords a condition binding them, under pain of forfeiture, to make "certain estates to their tenants at certain rents." Thus the system of tenancies-at-will was not only indirectly discouraged, but absolutely prohibited.[6] In this way it was that Chichester succeeded in establishing "fixity of tenure" in the North of Ireland in the reign of James I.

It now becomes important to inquire how the Ulster custom, as we find it existing to-day, was evolved out of the system of "certain estates at certain rents," established in the North of Ireland nearly three centuries ago. For the Ulster custom is not merely a system of "fixity of tenure;" it has other distinguishing features.

As the English Government had broken faith with the "natives," so the English landlords violated in many cases the terms of their grants, and refused to make "certain estates" to their tenants. This produced great dissatisfaction amongst the tenant classes. They began to "agitate." Some of the English tenants returned home, declining to hold farms upon the

[6] *Vide* Carte's "Life of Ormond I." 13th ed. 1736; and Appendix to Dr. Brewer's "Introduction to the Carew Calendar of State Papers," 1603—1624, p. 45.

new conditions which the Anglo-Irish landlords were endeavouring to impose upon them. As a collateral consequence of this departure, a few of the Irish began to move from the "waste lands," seeking to fill the places vacated by the English. The Irish had no other "home" to go to but the land in which they dwelt, and to which they were fondly attached. They were prepared to accept from the landlords terms which the free-born and tolerably well-to-do Britons would not tolerate. Thus there was a likelihood of an Irish incursion upon the lands reserved for the English alone. At this the king became alarmed. No great invasion by the Irish of the lands intended for English tenants had as yet taken place; but such an invasion might, it was conjectured, at any moment occur. What would then become of the "plantation"? At the very root of this project lay the determination to destroy that system of tenancies-at-will against which Davis had so strongly inveighed. It was for this that Chichester had worked, and planned, and schemed; and yet, after all, the system of tenancies-at-will was actually beginning to spring up.

It was abundantly clear to the mind of the king that if the English tenants, forced by landlord injustice, fled from Ireland, the Irish might move *en masse* from the "lean" lands, and would be only

too delighted to occupy the "fat" as tenants-at-will,
or upon almost any terms. This was to be prevented at all hazards.

In 1618 Captain Pynnar, a tried and valued
servant of the Crown, was despatched to Ulster, to
inquire into and to report upon the state of affairs
in the province. Captain Pynnar found things in
a very unsatisfactory condition. Almost everywhere the landlords were violating the terms of
their grants. They were not erecting buildings or
making improvements to the extent which had
been expected of them. These things were being
done by the tenants, whose tenure was nevertheless uncertain. Pynnar notes and complains of
this uncertainty of tenure very much in his report.[7]
" No [certain] estates, all his tenants from year to
year," is his commentary of the condition of things
which he found upon one property. Of the tenure
on another estate—that of Sir Claud Hamilton—
he says, " No [certain] estates as yet, but promises ;
not one freeholder." Again, " No freeholders, no
leases, no estates." He visits the property of a Mr.
Blennerhasset and reports, " Saw no freeholders ;
undertakers [landlords] in England, when I
came suddenly upon them " (the tenants). In
another place he observes, "undertakers [land-

---

[7] Pynnar's Survey, " Carew Calendar of State Papers,"
1603—1624, p. 393 *et seq.*

lords] out of the country; land well planted."
Next he reports what he saw upon the estate of Mr.
Cuthbert Cunningham. " Nothing built by him,
but sufficiently peopled with tenants, who build
after their manner." Pynnar adds, that the landlord "must build, and must answer for not
having already done so." He then comes upon
the territories of the Duke of Lennox, and reports,
" Here is built a strong castle of lime and stone,
but as yet no freeholders. The Duke of Lennox
is to answer to the king. I saw the land well
inhabited and full of people. What estates they
have I know not, neither would he [the lord] call
the tenants together; but he showed the counterpart of one lease, and says that each tenant has the
like"—a statement which Captain Pynnar seems
to have taken with considerable reservation. Upon
another property (Sir John Dromond's) he finds
affairs no better. " Many tenants (British) on the
land. They, knowing that I was in the county,
came and complained that for many years they
could never get anything but promises, and are for
the most part leaving. I desired the lady to show
me the counterparts [of the leases]. Her answer
was that her knight was in Scotland, and that he
could not come to them." Passing to the property of Earl Castlehaven, the " Royal Commissioner" observes that there are " no buildings and

no freeholders. I planted," he says, "some few English, but they have no estates; for, since the old earl died, they cannot have their leases made good unless they give treble the rent paid, and yet must have but half the land which they enjoyed in the late earl's time." With reference to the occurrences on other lands adjoining, Pynnar continues : " The agent showed me the rent-roll of tenants on these proportions, but the estates are so weak and uncertain that all are leaving ;" and he adds that the "Irish are coming in, contrary to the stipulations." Pynnar then proceeds to report generally that the tenants, both English and Irish, neglected to cultivate the soil properly, neither "ploughing nor using husbandry nor tillage," because they were " uncertain of their stay." " The British," he says, " who have built houses at their own charges have no estates, which is such a discouragement that they are minded to depart," and he winds up by stating that, "without a better settlement, these British will go elsewhere."[8]

The seriousness of the state of affairs thus reported by Pynnar, James thoroughly appreciated. He had set his heart upon the success of the Ulster "plantation," and there now seemed to be imminent danger of the whole work falling to pieces. To the fatality attendant upon the existence of a

[8] *Vide* Pynnar's " Survey," p. 723.

system of tenancies-at-will, the example of Munster bore testimony, and James wisely felt that if this system was not crushed at its very inception in Ulster, the great labours of Chichester and of Davis would be of no avail. The crisis was a grave one, but the king was equal to it. From the report of Pynnar he found that the landlords were the cause of the evils which were arising, and upon them his judgment fell. The patents of the incriminated proprietors became forfeited, and their estates, to use a modern stereotyped phrase, were "confiscated."

We now arrive at a crucial stage of the "evolution" of the Ulster custom. Here a very important question arises, upon the answer to which a good deal will, I think, turn with reference to the origin of the Ulster custom. The question is, what became of the lands which (1) were taken from the defaulting landlords, and (2) of the lands which the British tenants left, because they could not obtain security of tenure?

The lands of the defaulting landlords were, in some cases, I believe, left to the tenants who had built upon and improved them.

The lands or farms of the British tenants fell, I am disposed to think, mainly into the hands of the Scotch settlers. Out of the transactions which arose with reference to the passing of those farms from the British to the Scotch tenants, the Ulster custom of tenant right, as we see it existing in the north of Ireland to-day, sprang.

In what follows let me frankly say that I am entering upon a region of speculation, but with, as I think, very good guides.

Whatever merits or demerits this part of my work may possess, I can, at all events, say that I have approached the subject in an impartial spirit, and with an open mind. I started with no theory. Such researches as I have made were pursued, not with the view of sustaining a foregone conclusion, but of arriving at a judgment free from predilection.

At first the thought flashed upon my mind, suggested by something I had read, that the Ulster custom was of a growth anterior to the plantation period. But this view, I soon found, could not be maintained. I accordingly dismissed it at once from my mind, though natural and national predispositions would, I confess, have encouraged me to favour such a theory.

I next was inclined to think that the custom had been directly established by the plantation scheme, and that Chichester and Davis had it—or something like it—in their minds when formulating their plans. But this view I found to be as untenable as the first. It became quite clear to my mind that neither Chichester nor Davis ever sought to establish, or contemplated the springing up in the future, of any usage akin to the Ulster custom. What they both sought to, and did in a measure, establish, was " fixity of tenure "—" certain estates at certain rents." [9]　But this alone is not the Ulster custom.

This custom grew out of the occurrences which took place in consequence of the efforts made by the landlords, in the reign of James I., to break down the system of " fixity of tenure " created by the Lord Deputy and the Attorney General. The custom began to spring up, and was, in all probability, actually practised, in some few cases, between the years 1618 and 1620.

It was originated mainly by the Scotch tenants.

I shall now endeavour to state the reasons which have induced me to come to this conclusion. We learn from Pynnar that on his arrival in Ulster he found the English and the Irish, but especially the English tenants, discontented. Many of the latter had left, and others were threatening to leave, because they could not obtain certainty of tenure.[1] Now we have no evidence of similar discontent existing amongst the Scotch. On the contrary, there are reasons for supposing that they were tolerably well satisfied with the condition of things.

[9] *Vide* ante, p. 150.　　　　　[1] *Vide* ante, p. 155.

How was this ? it will be asked, and I think the matter is capable of easy explanation. The Irish
were, not unnaturally, dissatisfied with the way in
which the plantation scheme was turning out.
They had been driven from the "fat" to the
"lean" lands, and they saw strangers occupying
the rich pastures forbidden them. But it had been
expressly stipulated, by way of a compensating
balance, that they should have "fixity of tenure"
for their holdings. "Fixity of tenure," in the sense
of fixity of individual location, they certainly had
not under the Irish tribal system. Although under
that system the tribe, or clan, possessed rights
in the land superior to those of the chief himself, yet
an individual member of the sept, subject so largely
to the power of the chief, may be said to have
been in a certain sense a tenant-at-will. Now it
was the great desire of Davis to place the Irish
tenants in a better position, with respect to tenure
under the king, than, as he thought, they had
enjoyed under their former lords.[2] This "fixity of
tenure" was, in point of fact, a sort of bribe offered
to the Irish tenants to stand by the king, and to
desert their own chiefs. But when the plantation
scheme was completed, when the Irish tenants had
moved to the "lean" lands, consoling themselves—
so far as consolation was possible—with the reflection

[2] *Vide* ante, p. 66.

that they had, at all events, "certainty of tenure,' the English and the Anglicized Irish landlords, broke through the stipulations, and reintroduced the old system of tenancies-at-will — *minus* the rights of ownership formerly associated with it. The Irish tenants might have been prepared to put up with a system of tenancies-at-will under landlords who were, like themselves Irishmen, but they did not relish the idea of living at the mercy of a foreign proprietary. A " fellow-feeling " might have made Irish landlords " wondrous kind," even to tenants-at-will, but that feeling was not to be looked for amongst the " Saxon invaders." Hence the new system of tenancies-at-will was regarded by the natives as an unmitigated evil, and very naturally gave rise to much dissatisfaction amongst them. Those of their number who had been fortunate enough to get into the fat lands were at first contented to remain as tenants-at-will, but they in time became dissatisfied too.

With respect to the English tenants, they were discontented for equally obvious, though different, reasons. They had come from a rich and prosperous land, where certainty of tenure prevailed. They had been accustomed to good treatment, and they were determined not to put up with bad. Their only inducements for coming to Ireland were that they would receive good lands (perhaps a little better than many of them held in England) at a very much cheaper rent, and upon the same conditions, as to certainty of tenure, which existed in England.

But when they observed that these conditions were violated, when, having laid out their capital in buildings and other improvements, they found their properties and themselves placed at the mercy of the landlords, the inducements which had tempted them to migrate ceased. They had no longer certainty of tenure. The landlords might at six months' notice dismiss them, and " confiscate " their improvements. Their all had been invested in the land, and yet they could not call a rood of it their own for more than a twelvemonth. This certainly was a state of things not to be tolerated. The English tenants did not tolerate it. They resolved at once, as we have seen, to depart from the colony, and to return to their own country, where they could be sure of fair play and honest dealing.[3]

The Scotch stood in a different position. They had come from the worst parts of a land upon which Gibbon says the Romans declined to advance, because " the masters of the fairest and most wealthy climates of the globe turned with contempt from gloomy hills, assailed by the winter tempest ; from lakes concealed in a blue mist ; and from cold

[3] *Vide* ante, p. 155.

M

and lonely heaths, over which the deer of the forest were chased by a troop of naked barbarians."[4] The Scotch who came to Ireland in the reign of James I. were an impoverished and destitute class. We have it upon the authority of the State Papers that for months after their arrival they were practically supported by the Irish. The condition oi those Scotch settlers in Ulster might not have been all that they desired ; but the likelihood is that they were much better off there than they had been, or could very well expect to be, at home. Hence it was that they did not exhibit the inclination which the English had shown, under altered and untoward circumstances, of returning to their own country.

Although, as I have observed, the Scotch were for some time after their arrival in Ulster chiefly supported by the Irish, a change soon took place in their fortunes. They gradually began to do well—so well, indeed, that when Pynnar came, in 1618, he found that the North Britons, instead oi being supported by the Irish, were themselves supporting both the Irish and the English.

"Many English," says Pynnar, "do not plough or use husbandry, being fearful to stock themselves with cattle or servants for those labours.

---

[4] Gibbon's "Decline and Fall of the Roman Empire," vol. i. p. 141.

Neither do the Irish use tillage, for they are also uncertain of their stay. So by these means—the Irish using grazing only, and the English very little—were it not for the Scottish, who plough in many places, the rest of the country might starve. By reason of this the British, who are forced to take their lands at great rates, live at the greater rents paid them by the Irish tenants who graze."[s]

What seems to have taken place was this:— The English, having at first erected buildings, cultivated the soil, and generally improved the land, suddenly desisted from their exertions, and refrained from incurring further risks by outlay of capital or otherwise, on finding that they could not obtain security of tenure. They then appear simply to have let their lands to the Irish for grazing purposes, charging high rents for the same. The Irish, on the other hand, it may, I think, be gathered, used those lands for keeping and rearing stock, which they in all probability subsequently sold to the Scotch. The Scotch at this time, I am disposed to conclude, were the tenants who chiefly farmed in tillage, planted, carried on dairy operations, and, in a word, did the ordinary cultivator's work. Is it too violent a proposition to submit that the Scotch, who had thus begun to

[s] Pynnar's Survey, " Carew Calendar of State Papers (Ireland)," 1603—1624, p. 423.

acquire a good position in the province, and were
contented to remain there, should have kept their
eyes on the lands of the English, who were determined to go away?   Those English and Scotch
tenants were constantly thrown together in the
daily relations of life.   How natural that they
should have often discussed the situation.   How
probable that the English tenants should have complained to their Scotch neighbours, as we know they
afterwards complained to Pynnar, of the want of
security of tenure ?[6]   Is it not possible to conceive
some discontented English tenant, or a number of
such tenants, expressing his or their determination
to give up their farms and to leave the land ?   How
would the Scotch be likely to receive such intel-
ligence?   What more conceivable, in such circumstances, than that the Englishman should
demand a *quid pro quo* for the possession ?   Such
a demand the Scotchman could not well consider unreasonable, and in all probability some
bargain for the transfer of the possession of the
English farms to the Scotch tenants would
ultimately be arrived at between them.   It is
clear, from Pynnar's "Survey," that the English
were anxious to leave, and the frugal Scots
would not unnaturally have traded upon this
anxiety.[7]

[6] *Vide* ante, p. 154.   [7] *Vide* ante, p. 155.

And thus a transaction for the sale of the Englishman's interest in the possession of his farm would be brought about.

It is my impression—my theory—that a series of such transactions took place in Ulster between the years 1617 and 1620. Another matter worthy of consideration is, that transactions of this nature would have readily been countenanced—probably encouraged—by Pynnar, and for the following reasons. The English having once determined to give up their farms, and to leave the country, a question of considerable importance would arise as to what should become of those farms. They could not be permitted to lie waste. That is clear. Only two other alternatives remained. Those farms should be given either to the Irish, or to the Scotch. Pynnar would not be likely to accept the first alternative, for the lands were not only " fat " —and from the " fat " lands the Irish were to be excluded—but they were also well situated for warlike purposes, if war should ever arise between the settlers and natives. The second alternative remained, and this, naturally, both Pynnar and the king would be well disposed to adopt. I believe this alternative was adopted, and that the Scotch occupied the vacated English lands, paying a certain sum for the possession, or for what, in modern phraseology, we should call the " good-will." This practice of one tenant taking the land of another—paying so much for the former's "goodwill"—grew slowly, imperceptibly. Exercised at first in a few isolated cases, it gradually developed, during the progress of years, into a general custom, extending step by step from one part of a county to the rest, then from county to county of the "plantation" counties at first, and lastly spreading to other districts beyond the "settlement." In the earlier stages of its advancement, I think it may be taken that the landlords offered no opposition to this custom. They were too much in disgrace in the days of Pynnar to make their influence, however adversely used, much felt. That they did at this time use their influence adversely to the development of the custom, I have no reason for supposing. Most probably they did not. The custom stole a march upon them. It was a *fait accompli* in many parts of a county before the landlords knew where they were, and it spread with beneficial acceleration. In more modern days, however, when the custom had assumed formidable proportions, and when landlords began to think that the independence which the tenants enjoyed under it, might militate against the exercise of their prerogatives, a stand was attempted to be made against what was now called the "tenants' right." But in the struggle which ensued the tenants held their own. The battle between landlord and tenant in Ulster was fought out upon more equal terms than that battle had been contested in Munster and in Connaught. No English Government had attempted to back up the landlords of the north, against the Protestant tenants of the north, as all the Governments of England, from the time of Elizabeth to that of Victoria, had backed up the landlords of the south against the Catholic tenants of the south. Ulster was not perpetually governed by Insurrection Acts and martial law. The tenants of Ulster were habitually allowed to bear arms, and to combine as the free citizens of a free State. And, by arms, and combinations they asserted and preserved the Ulster Custom.[8]

The Ulster Custom, in its present form, may be said to consist of two main features :—

(1) Permissive fixity of tenure.

(2) The tenant's right to sell the good-will of his farm.

With respect to the first, Judge Longfield says : " It is expected that as long as the tenant

[8] *Vide* Gordon's " History of Ireland," and the evidence of Mr. Porter, Mr. McCarter, and Mr. Henderson before the Devon Commission.

pays his rent the landlord will not use his legal powers to put an end to the tenancy."

With respect to the second, the same learned authority adds : " If a tenant finds it necessary, or convenient to leave his farm he may sell his tenant right, with the approbation of the landlord. This approbation is not to be capriciously refused, but, on the other hand, the tenant is not at liberty to select any substitute that he thinks proper, irrespective of his character, and possession of sufficient means for the efficient cultivation of the land."[9]

It is this latter feature which gives to the Ulster Custom its great distinguishing characteristic, though the principle of fixity of tenure is likewise indigenous to the soil of the north. I shall give an instance of the way in which this custom worked previously to the passing of Mr.

---

[9] *Vide* Judge Longfield's paper on " The Tenure of Land in Ireland." (" Cobden Club Essays," pp. 39, 40.) Mr. Handcock, an extensive land agent in the province of Ulster, thus defines tenant right :—" Tenant right I consider to be the claim of the tenant and his heirs to continue in undisputed possession of the farm so long as the rent is paid ; and, in case of an ejectment, or in the event of a change of occupancy at the wish of either landlord or tenant, it is the sum of money which the new occupier pays to the old one for the peaceable enjoyment of his holding."— Mr. Handcock, as quoted by Mr. Butt, in his " Land Tenure in Ireland," p. 50.

Gladstone's Land Act, in 1870. Let me suppose that Donald McFarlane, owing to bad seasons, and for other reasons, falls into arrears of rent. Pressed for payment, he goes to the landlord, and asks for a reduction, or additional time to pay. The landlord refuses, saying, "You already owe two or three years' rent. I cannot wait any longer. Neither is it possible for me to give, or reasonable on your part to ask for, a reduction. If you cannot pay the rent of the farm, then your course is clear. Sell your tenant right. You know that you will get as much, and perhaps more, for it than I would for the fee simple." [1]

To an argument of this kind it is difficult for Donald McFarlane successfully to reply.

He cannot reasonably expect a reduction of his rent, and the recognition of his tenant right by the landlord at the same time.

And if he were, for a temporary advantage, to accept the first, at the sacrifice of the second, he would be doing a permanent injury to his interests. In addition he would, by adopting such a course, be certain to turn local public opinion, upon which, in such circumstances, the landlord could rely,

---

[1] Lord Dufferin once said that in many parts of the north, under the Ulster custom, the tenant's saleable interest in his farm frequently fetched a sum considerably beyond the price of the landlord's fee simple of it.

against him. Thus no alternative is practically left to Donald McFarlane but to bow to the decision of the landlord, and this he accordingly does. He then looks around for a purchaser, meets one, and a bargain is quickly struck up for the sale of the tenant right. Then both tenants proceed to the agent for his approval or opinion of the contract, and the agent, if reasonably satisfied that the incoming tenant is a fairly solvent and respectable man, gives his sanction to the bargain.[2] Donald McFarlane's name is then immediately removed from the books, and that of the incoming tenant, he having previously paid all arrears of rent due by his predecessor, takes its place. Thus, to use the words of Judge Longfield, "the transaction is completed without any law expenses, or any risk of title."[3]

For some forty or fifty years past the Ulster landlords have been encroaching upon, restricting, and resisting the Ulster tenant right custom. But the Ulster tenants have met their efforts with strenuous and persistent opposition. They have contested the matter in the law courts, and let me

[2] " The right which the landlord has, on the sale of a tenant right, to object to the purchaser or the price is very rarely exercised." (Judge Longfield, "Cobden Club Essays," First Series, p. 44.)

[3] "The Tenure of Land in Ireland." ("Cobden Club Essays," First Series, p. 41.)

add they have occasionally, and with greater effect, taken the law into their own hands.

I am afraid my English readers will not be disposed to believe that the Ulster tenants have ever taken the law into their own hands. I must allow no doubts to exist upon the point. " Have there been any agrarian outrages in your district ?" Mr. Porter, a Presbyterian clergyman, was asked, before the Devon Commission. He replied : " There are just three instances in which there were agrarian outrages committed since I settled in this county, and these originated in the total denial of tenant right." [4]

Mr. Handcock, the agent of Lord Lurgan, says, " If systematic attempts were made amongst the proprietors of Ulster to invade tenant right, I do not believe there is a force at the disposal of the Horse Guards sufficient to keep the peace of the province." [5]

Another witness, examined before the Devon Commission—Mr. Lindsay, landed proprietor—says, " Some [landlords] recognize it [tenant right], and some do not ; but where they do not recognize it, and set their face against it, they are very generally defeated, and have been obliged to do it, after risking life in some instances, in my neighbour-

---

[4] *Vide* " Digest of Devon Commission," part i. p. 296.
[5] *Vide* " Digest of Devon Commission," part i. p. 303.

hood." [6]   Mr. Lindsay adds, " A landlord put a man out of his farm.   He (the landlord) sent down a person to cultivate the farm, and he (the new tenant) was sent home again.   The people gathered that night, and desired him to go home, and not come there again ; and the tenant got leave to sell his tenant right afterwards." [7]

I have now endeavoured to state what the Ulster custom is, and have attempted to trace its origin. The question remains for consideration—" What are its results ? "

[6] " Digest of Devon Commission," part i. p. 303.
[7] " Digest of Devon Commission," part i. *ibid.*

VII.

THE ULSTER CUSTOM.

PART II.: RESULTS.

THERE seems to be but one opinion as to the results of the Ulster custom, amongst most persons who have given attention to the question, viz. that the system works beneficially wherever it prevails. I shall content myself in this chapter with merely placing before my readers a few brief extracts from some of the statements which have been made by several men of authority, from time to time, upon the subject.

Mr. Leslie Foster, Ulster landlord :—" I attribute the great difference between the province of Ulster and the other counties in Ireland to the settlement of James I. . . . Wherever the tenants have a beneficial and substantial interest, there are no disturbances. They have such an interest in Ulster."[1]

[1] *Vide* Select Committee (House of Lords) on the State of Ireland, p. 58.

Mr. Kinmouth, farmer :—" It [the custom] gives the tenant an interest in the land, and encourages him to improve."[2]

Mr. Andrews, agent :—" In the state of things in Ireland, with our small farms, there is no other means of securing the improvement of land, and giving confidence to the tenants, but recognizing the tenant right." . . . " I think the curtailment of tenant right cannot be carried out without danger to the peace of the country. You would have a Tipperary in Down if it was attempted to be carried out."[3]

Mr. McCullogh, agent:—" The system gives satisfaction generally to the farmers."[4]

Mr. Lowry, farmer:—" The denial of tenant right creates very great dissatisfaction. The tenants have ceased to improve as they would have done."[5]

Mr. Orr, farmer :—" The general feeling in the country is very much opposed to an alteration of the custom. It is creating very general excitement, and it operates as a check to improvement."[6]

Mr. Lindsay, landlord.[7]

---

[2] " Digest of Devon Commission," part i. p. 294.
[3] Ibid., p. 300.   [4] Ibid., p. 301.
[5] Ibid., p. 301.   [6] Ibid., p. 302.
[7] *Vide* ante, p. 171.

Mr. Henry Murray, agent :—" The system of allowing the incoming tenant to purchase the interest of the outgoing tenant prevents a large arrear accruing upon the estate" (for), "if there is an arrear it is usually paid off"[8] (by the incoming tenant).

Mr. William Stuart French, agent :—" It has some beneficial effect in preventing agrarian outrages."[9]

Mr. McCarthy, middleman :—" It has generally a good effect."[1]

Mr. Richard Byrne, farmer :—" The effect is rather beneficial, for where an improvident person disposes of his tenant right, the landlord gets a person more likely to improve the farm."[2]

Mr. Sinclair, landlord :—" I am sure [the custom] gives confidence to improving tenants." .. . "I think the custom is a very valuable and useful custom."[3]

Mr. Senior, the late Commissioner of Poor Laws, says, "I attribute almost entirely to the custom of tenant right, both the absence of agrarian outrage in the north, as well as a much higher cultivation in that part of the country."[4]

---

[8] " Digest of Devon Commission," part i. p. 304.
[9] Ibid., p. 306. [1] Ibid., p. 309.
[2] Ibid., p. 312. [3] Ibid., p. 318.
[4] Mr. Nassau Senior, as quoted in Mr. Butt's " Land Tenure in Ireland," p. 53.

Mr. Handcock, agent :—" Much of Ulster's prosperity has been the result of this extraordinary matter (namely, tenant right) in connexion with tenure, and no measure would have a greater effect in improving the condition of the south and west than the introduction of tenant right as it exists in Ulster.

   *   *   *   *   *

" I consider tenant right beneficial to the community, because it establishes a security in the possession of land, and leads to the improvement of the estate, without any expenditure of capital on the part of the landlord. It likewise affords the best security for his rent, as arrears are always allowed to be deducted from the amount the occupier receives for tenant right. It is very conducive to the peace of the country, for almost every man has a stake in the community, and is, therefore, opposed to agrarian outrages as well as riots. Laws are more respected ; there are none of those reckless, daring men who are ready for any deed, under the consciousness that their situation cannot be worse ; the liberty of the subject is more respected ; an imprisonment has greater terrors, from the fact that almost any tenant can procure bail for his future appearance in court, or his future good behaviour. There is never any instance of forfeited recognizance. An arrest is, therefore, a much more serious matter in this than in other parts of Ireland ; for as there is less risk (from his stake) of the offender flying, so here the degradation is more keenly felt, and parties often subscribe, and bring actions against magistrates, for false arrest and imprisonment ; whereas, where no tenant right exists, the first step is the arrest, to prevent escape, and secondly, the consideration of the cause. Imprisonment and contamination with bad characters are thus more frequent. The magistrates cannot have the same respect for the liberty of the subject ; and when acts of oppression occur, revenge is taken, not by an appeal to the civil court for damages, but by combination and an appeal to force, waylaying, and murder. The necessity of distress for rent—a fruitful source of riots and broken heads—is also obviated by the tenant right, as there is no danger of loss of arrears. The landlords are compelled to recognize tenant right, as in several instances in this neighbourhood, where they have refused to allow tenant right, the incoming tenant's house has been burned, his cattle houghed, or his crops trodden down by night. The disallowance of tenant right, as far as I know, is always attended with outrage. A landlord cannot even resume possession to himself without paying for it. In fact, it is one of the sacred rights of the country which cannot be touched with im-

N

punity ; and if systematic efforts were made amongst the proprietors of Ulster to invade tenant right, I do not believe there is a force at the disposal of the Horse Guards sufficient to keep the peace of the province ; and when we consider that all the improvements have been effected at the expense of the tenant, it is perfectly right that this tenant right should exist ; his money has been laid out on the faith of the compensation in that shape. I think it also affords facilities for the introduction of a better class of farmers, and tends to consolidation, because portions of land can be purchased, and large farms made, without disturbing the goodwill of the community." [5]

Captain Kennedy, the Secretary to the Devon Commission, thus sums up the evidence given before the Commissioners on this subject. "In the north of Ireland," he says, "this system is pretty generally either authorized, or connived at by the landlord ; and it is not uncommon for a tenant without a lease to sell the bare privilege of occupancy, or possession of his farm, without any visible sign of improvement having been made by him, at from ten to sixteen, and up to twenty and

---

[5] *Vide* Hancock's evidence, as quoted by Daniel O'Connell in the House of Commons, April 3, 1846. *Vide* O'Connell's Collected Speeches by M. F. Cusack, p. 203, also "Digest of the Devon Commission," part i. p. 295.

even forty years' purchase of the rent; and the comparative tranquillity of that district may, perhaps, be mainly attributable to this fact. . . .

"In the north, where it is permitted, agrarian crimes are rare. In other places, where it is resisted, they are of common occurrence. Landowners do not perceive that the disorganized state of Tipperary, and the agrarian combination throughout Ireland, are but methodized war to obtain the Ulster tenant right, or that an established practice not only may, but must, erect itself finally into law." [6]

The Report of the Devon Commission says, " Anomalous as this custom is, if considered with reference to all ordinary notions of property, it must be admitted that the district in which it prevails has thriven and improved, in comparison with other parts of the country ; and although we can foresee some danger to the just rights of property from the unlimited allowance of this ' tenant right,' yet we are sure that evils more immediate, and of still greater magnitude, would result from any hasty or general disallowance of it." [7]

Judge Longfield says, " In Ulster, free trade in land, as far as the right of occupation is concerned,

[6] *Vide* " Introduction to Digest of Devon Commission," part i. pp. 1—4.
[7] " Digest of the Devon Commission," part ii. p. 1120.

prevails in the most perfect manner. . . . Under this system the tenantry cannot be very poor. . . . To the manager of an estate the system is very agreeable. The rents are moderate, and paid punctually, and the agent is not subjected to the harassing labour and danger which attend the enforcement of rent in many parts of Ireland. There are no evictions by process of law, but if the tenant is not thriving, and finds it difficult to pay his rent, he is warned by the agent, or his own prudence, that he ought to sell his tenant right, and retire from his farm with a good sum in hand to emigrate, or support him in some other pursuit, before he is totally ruined, by remaining in a farm that he is unable to cultivate with profit. He is succeeded by a wealthier, or more skilful, tenant, and the landlord, and the country at large, gain by the change." [8]

Chief Justice Whiteside: " If the existence of what is called tenant right be productive of good in Ulster, the principle should be fearlessly applied to the other provinces." [9]

Lord Portsmouth : " More than half a century ago the Ulster custom with free sale (practically)

[8] " Land Tenure in Ireland." (" Cobden Club Essays," p. 44.)

[9] Chief Justice Whiteside, as quoted in Mr. Butt's " Land Tenure," p. 52.

was introduced on my estate in the County Wexford. The results are the same as in the County Down, and wherever the custom exists, viz. a well-to-do tenantry."[1]

Lord Lymington: " The Portsmouth tenant right was introduced in the year 1822, by the late Lord Portsmouth, with the able assistance of Mr. Nicholas Ellis, who was at that time agent, and whose thorough acquaintance with Irish character and requirements enabled him to co-operate with success in the establishment of a new form of administration considerably in advance of public opinion. From that time up to the present mutual confidence, respect, and kindliness have steadily grown in the relationship between landlord and tenant.

* * * *

" On this estate, where the above mentioned system has been tried for thirty-seven years, there has been no case of eviction from an agricultural holding in the sense of the tenant being removed and the farm passing to the landlord. There have been three cases of ejectment in twelve years, in the sense of a tenant being unable to pay rent and declining to sell ; but in each of these cases the tenant was allowed a free sale after the sheriff had taken possession, the incoming tenant was

[1] *Times,* July 15, 1880.

accepted, the arrears paid to the landlord, and the tenant received a handsome balance.

"It may be summed up, therefore, that this experiment of fifty-eight years' trial has been proved just and equal, because it has resulted in general contentment and material advantage to landlord and tenant. The landlord can with justice feel proud of an independent and prosperous tenantry."[2]

The truth, in a word, is that wherever the Ulster custom is established, peace and prosperity prevail.

I have said elsewhere[3] that I believe the people of Ireland will now accept no settlement of the Land Question which does not include a scheme for the establishment of a peasant proprietary. This is my view still.

It is the opinion of those who, in a large degree, possess the confidence of the Irish people, that strong measures ought to be taken, and taken promptly, to bring about this end. The expropriation of the landlords has been spoken of. It has been said, "there is not room in Ireland for both landlord and tenants. If either must go, the landlords must go." This has not been the

---

[2] *The Nineteenth Century*, Oct. 1880, and *Vide* Appendix E.
[3] "The Irish Land Question and English Public Opinion."

first time that the statement has been advanced
that Ireland is too small for her population.
But in former times it was always declared that the
tenants must go ; and the tenants have gone, as the
Times once said, " with a vengeance." In every
struggle between the tenants and the landlords
in the past, the tenants have gone to the wall.
The Irish people—the Irish nation—have gone
to the wall. Can it then be wondered at that
a reaction should now set in, and that the cry
should at last be sent forth, the landlords must
go ?

Suppose the Normans had never become English
in spirit ; suppose England were governed from
Paris to-day, and that a Catholic landocracy,
differing in " race and religion " from the people
of this country, and opposed to them in National sympathies and wishes, were possessed
of all the land, whilst the English Protestant
tenants groaned under a system which had made
them beggars and serfs ; suppose in such a
case that the question arose whether the English
millions or the Norman lords should go,—how
would an Englishman answer it ? How would
Cromwell have answered it ? How did he answer the
question whether the king should die, or the people
be oppressed ? When James II. was suspected of
attempting to do in England what the Irish land-

lords have been encouraging and driving on the Governments of England to do in Ireland for nearly 300 years, viz., to exclude from power and position those who professed the National faith, and represented the National sentiment, what became of him? What has become of every man, and of every body of men in history, who have aroused the popular fury by unjustly and unwisely denying the popular demands? Writing on the 11th March, 1848, to Baron Stockmar, the late Prince Consort said, "The state of things in Germany is very remarkable, and is another proof that what does not happen at the right time is, by force of circumstances, sooner or later brought to pass, and then with a crash."[4] Justice is always done in the end, and whether it is effected by extreme or moderate measures of reform always depends upon the attitude assumed by those who endeavour to retard or defeat it. The demands of the Irish tenants are "extreme" to-day, because justice was not done them "at the right time."

Mr. Parnell has been frequently asked to state his views for the settlement of the Irish Land Question. But beyond giving it as his opinion that a peasant proprietary ought to be established, he has for some time declined to commit himself

---

[4] Theodore Martin's "Life of the Prince Consort," vol. ii. p. 14.

further to details. His reasons for this silence would seem to have been, that the tenants have over and over again made proposals for the reform of what is admitted, on all hands, to be a bad system ; that their proposals have always met with hostile criticism and failure ; that the land-lords have never made any proposals at all ; encountering every attempt at a settlement with a dogged *non possumus*, or by a mere cry of confiscation and communism. Mr. Parnell has said it must now be the turn of the landlords "to bid ; " the tenants have made offers enough ; they will make no more. However, yielding at last to frequent importunities, he has indicated the means which, in his opinion, ought to be employed to create a peasant proprietary in Ireland.

His suggestion is this, that the tenants should be allowed to extinguish the rent, and become proprietors of their holdings, on the payment for thirty-five years of a Government valuation rent.

This is certainly an "extreme measure." Any measure which compels a man to give up his property, whether he likes it or not, is extreme, and can only be justified on the grounds of public necessity and the public good. But, where such necessity exists, and where the interests of the community demand the interference on the part of the State with the rights of individuals, the act has always been held to be perfectly justifiable.

Instances of such interference take place every day. I need only allude to the common case of expropriating a landowner, through whose estate it is deemed essential, for the public good, that a railway should run.

Mr. Parnell's plan for expropriating the Irish landlords, and creating a peasant proprietary after thirty-five years' payment by the tenants of a Government valuation rent, may be difficult of attainment, or not—may be within the range of practical politics at the present moment, or not; but if the necessity for its adoption exists on political and economical grounds, it certainly rests upon equitable and well recognized principles of law and morality.

Mr. Bright's proposal for the establishment of a peasant proprietary in Ireland is, I take it, familiar to the great majority of my readers. Mr. Parnell's plan is, as we have seen, compulsory. Mr. Bright's is enabling. It is this; that the State should be authorized to advance two-thirds (or three-fourths, as originally proposed) of the purchase-money to tenants desirous of buying their holdings from landlords willing to sell.

Mr. Bright's scheme has been tried, but has not, up to the present, been a success, chiefly because the machinery employed for working it is wholly unfitted for the purpose. This machinery is the Landed Estates Court.

The business of this Court is to sell estates, and to give good titles—not to make peasant proprietors. But this is not all. The action of the department is not merely neutral—and neutrality in the matter would be bad enough—it is positively a hindrance to the creation of a peasant proprietary. No facilities whatever are afforded intending peasant purchasers; whilst the mode in which the estates passing through the Court are offered for sale presents insurmountable obstacles to the accomplishment of the tenants' efforts.

It was, I conceive, the object, and intention of Mr. Bright when he framed those clauses, that, the estates coming into the market should be put up for sale in such lots as would not only make it convenient for tenants to become proprietors, but would invite and encourage them so to become. But what has happened? The estates, instead of being divided for the purposes of sale into small lots, such as ten, fifteen, or twenty acres, have been sold *en bloc*, that is to say, by the hundreds of acres. In such circumstances, all the tenants can do is to combine among themselves, and endeavour to raise a sum which will enable them to purchase the whole

property, and then redistribute it in small proportions amongst each other. But combinations of
this nature by humble farmers are difficult of
formation and success. Attempts at such peasant
syndicates nevertheless there have been ; and on
two or three occasions some strong friends in Dublin
have come forward to purchase those estates for
the tenants, with the object of ultimately redis-
tributing them in convenient proportions. I have
elsewhere[s] mentioned some cases in which a transaction of this kind occurred, and have shown that,
though vigorously worked, success was not attained, failure being mainly caused by the unfitness
of the Landed Estates Court as a department for
facilitating the *creating* of a peasant proprietary.

What then is to be done ? Most assuredly if
the Bright clauses are to receive a fair trial, some
department must be especially created for the
purpose of working them. The sole business of
this department must be to facilitate and encourage the springing up of a peasant proprietary.
A head office should be established in Dublin,
and branches opened in every important agricultural centre throughout the country. Tenants
intending to purchase should find all the necessary
official information close at hand, and it should be
easily and cheaply obtainable. They should not be

[s] " Land Question and English Public Opinion," pp. 48—50.

compelled, as they now are, to come to Dublin at considerable expense, and there obliged either to employ a lawyer—a thing they cannot afford to do—or to seek out for themselves, from the officials of the Landed Estates Court, all essential particulars—a matter beyond their capacities. It cannot be expected that the officials of the Landed Estates Court will lose their time in assisting the peasants of Ireland to become proprietors. They are not paid for it. But it must be made the business and the interest of some Government department to see that an important Act of Parliament is not rendered "a dead letter" for want of adequate and efficacious machinery to make it thoroughly and actively operative.

A matter of paramount importance is the arrangement of the lots for sale. Wherever it is practicable the smaller those lots the better, a *minimum*, of course, to be fixed in all cases. Where it is necessary to offer the estate in large lots, or *en bloc*, the property should be purchased by the State—by the department I suggest—or by some associated company, assisted by Government aid. Some institution similar to the Rent Banks of the continent ought to be established.

By such a machinery the State could buy up the properties which the tenants would be unable to purchase, and sell them to the occupiers. As

M. Morier puts it, the object of the State in this matter being not to make money, but to create proprietors, without loss to itself, the principle of competition should not be allowed to act in these sales. Two conditions might be laid down : 1. That the farm should be of sufficient size fully to maintain the proprietor and his family according to the highest scale of comfort known in the district. 2. That the intended proprietor should possess the necessary capital to work it. When these conditions were fulfilled the actual occupier ought to have the right of pre-emption. By the adoption of some such means the Bright clauses may yet be made effective for the purposes to accomplish which they were enacted.

But there is a party in Ireland who are of opinion that it is not absolutely necessary to get rid of the landlords ; who think that there is still room in the country for both landlords and tenants, and that a *modus vivendi* may be arrived at between them, provided that the latter can obtain fixity or perpetuity of tenure at fair rents. The proposals for effecting this end are many. Foremost amongst them is the project for the extension of the Ulster custom to the whole of Ireland. It is argued that the existence of this custom in the north of Ireland has been attended with such signal benefits that its application to the south must lead to equally fortunate consequences. I do not think that the slightest doubt exists in the mind of any one conversant with Irish affairs, but that the extension of the Ulster custom throughout Ireland would be productive of satisfactory results. But it must not be forgotten that the Ulster custom possesses defects which, owing to the friendly relations that long subsisted between land-lord and tenant in Ulster, have not, happily, ope-rated injuriously to the welfare of the agricultural classes in that part of the kingdom. If, however, the custom be extended in its present form, and with these defects, to the other provinces, where the relations between landlord and tenant are not so friendly, it may prove inefficacious to bring about the condition of things desired.

The great defect in the Ulster custom is, that, while under no circumstances giving the tenant any right to a reduction, it permits the landlord so to increase the rent from time to time as almost to destroy the tenant's interests. The tenant has no remedy for the practical confiscation of his improvements which this rent raising may involve, unless he is evicted or quits his holding. He can then sell his good-will. That is his remedy. But as long as he chooses to remain in possession

—and often he has no alternative but to remain in possession—he is compelled to pay a penalty in the way of increased rent for his industry and outlay. However, in the north there is a strong local public opinion, and the tenants are very loyal to each other.[6] The result is a practical check upon unfair rent raising. In the south no similar check to landlord injustice will be found. There is not, in the southern districts, an equally strong local opinion to overawe landlord cupidity ; nor have the southern tenants been in the habit—owing to the terrible scramble for land amongst them—of combining to keep rents down to a fair margin.

Legislation, to be effective for the protection and security of those tenants who cannot, as I have already said, help themselves, must, by express enactment or procedure, render rack-renting absolutely impossible. The tenant must, in fact, be taken out of the power of the landlord. He

---

[6] " Although the Custom of Tenant Right has been established as a Custom by the moderation and fair dealing of the Ulster landlords, the loyalty of the tenantry to each other has contributed to its maintenance. A landlord who was considered to have treated an out-going tenant with injustice would find difficulty in getting another tenant to take the farm."—Lord Dufferin's Irish Emigration and the Tenure of Land in Ireland, p. 309. For Lord Dufferin's opinion on a system of Tenancy of Will, *vide* Appendix I.

must be made wholly independent, so long as he pays a fair rent, and does not injure or deteriorate the value of the land.

The difficulty is to decide what is a fair rent. How is it to be ascertained and fixed? The machinery generally suggested in Ireland for ascertaining a fair rent is, I believe, valuation by the State. Let the Government, it is said, value the land periodically, every twenty or thirty or forty years, and let the rent fixed by such valuation prevail for a given period. The objection taken to this proposal is that it involves State regulation of price in daily contracts between man and man. I do not think that this objection is insurmountable. It is certainly advisable that there should be as little State interference as possible in private or individual affairs. But a necessity may sometimes arise when the results produced by its non-interference might be infinitely more disastrous than any consequence which might follow from State interposition. It must not, either, be forgotten that there has been a good deal of State interference to assist the landlords in Ireland. There might be a little now to help the tenants—rather, to do justice to them. Of course, if it be possible to devise some procedure for fixing a fair rent which will obviate the necessity of such constant Government

O

intervention, it ought, unquestionably, to be preferred. Some such procedure has, in one or two notable instances, been adopted, and the circumstances are worthy of mention and consideration :—

In the year 1866, and again in 1870, differences arose between Captain Nolan and some tenants whom he had evicted in the county Galway. Captain Nolan proposed that the matters in dispute should be left to the arbitration of any three public men whom the tenants would name or be satisfied with.

All parties quickly agreed to the appointment of the following gentlemen as arbitrators : Sir John Gray, M.P., Father Lavelle, and Mr. A. M. Sullivan. After several days' deliberations, having held a public court on the spot, examined witnesses, and thoroughly investigated all the circumstances connected with the case, the arbitrators made an award acquitting Captain Nolan of all personal blame, though holding him legally accountable for the acts of his agents, and ordering that certain of the tenants who had been evicted should be restored to their old homesteads or placed in possession of new ones upon terms laid down in the award. Those terms were that Captain Nolan should grant to the tenants such a lease as the arbitrators would frame or approve of. The result was the Portacarron

Lease.[7] This document seems to have been framed, not with the view merely of adjusting the relations between Captain Nolan and his tenantry, but with the design, apparently, of indicating certain lines within which it might, in the future, be possible to formulate a scheme, or plan for dealing with the whole question of the tenure of land in Ireland. The provisions of the Portacarron Lease are briefly as follows :—

Term : 10,000 years. Rent : initial rent by valuation ; to be increasable or decreasable at the end of every ten years, according as the past ten years' average price of ten articles of farm produce rose or fell, as compared with the price of them at the date of the lease, endorsed on the back of the document.

Forfeiture for non-payment of rent.

      „   „ Subdivision.

      „   „ Subletting.

      „   „ Waste.

Reservations : game, woods, minerals, quarries, water-courses.

Such is the Portacarron Lease. It certainly possesses the merit of suggesting a practical course by the adoption of which a "fair rent" may be fixed, without Government action. I shall only add, that the lease has up to the present worked

[7] *Vide* Appendix F.

well, and that the relations between Captain Nolan and his Portacarron tenantry are now of the most friendly character.

The next instance is that which introduced what is called the Longfield Lease :—

Appreciating the great defect in the Ulster Custom to which I have alluded, Judge Longfield, in 1870, made a proposal for remedying it. I hardly think I can do better than state in the words of Professor Cairns what this proposal was, and his own views respecting it. " The plan," says Professor Cairns, is as follows : " It is proposed to confer on every tenant farmer in Ireland the right of purchasing a ' Parliamentary Tenant-Right ' at a certain number of years' purchase of his rent— we will say, for the purpose of illustration, seven. The purchase-money in case of an ordinary tenant from year to year would be made up of three elements. 1. A certain sum to be allowed for occupation right. 2. A certain sum in consideration of permanent improvements in the land. 3. The balance, which is to be paid in cash. Thus, supposing a tenant holding a farm of fifty acres at a rent of 1*l*. per acre, his Tenant-Right at seven years' purchase of the rental would amount to 350*l*., which might be made up as follows : Occupation right, valued, say, at two years' purchase, 100*l*. ; outlay on permanent improvements, 100*l*. ; cash,

150*l.* Price of ' Parliamentary Tenant-Right,' 350*l.*
In the case of a tenant in Ulster who had, on
getting possession of his farm, paid for the 'good-
will,' the sum paid for this would enter into the
price as a further element. The price of a ' Parliamentary Tenant-Right' for a similar farm of
fifty acres, would then be made up thus :—Occupation right at two years' purchase, 100*l.* ; payment
for good-will, 100*l.* ; permanent improvements not
covered by the good-will, 100*l.* ; cash, 50*l.* Price of
' Parliamentary Tenant-Right,' 350*l.* It is also a
part of the proposal that, where the tenant is
unable to pay the cash balance, the requisite sum
should be advanced to him by the Board of Public
Works, under conditions analogous to those laid
down in Parts 2 and 3 of the Government Bill. It
would, of course, in all cases be necessary, that
before obtaining his ' Parliamentary Tenant-Right '
he should establish his claims under the head of
' occupation right,' payment for 'good-will,' and
outlay on permanent improvements ; and it is
suggested that the cash balance should be expended
in improvements on the farm, or, where this was
not required, in reducing, on reasonable terms, the
rent. In the event of improvements being made
by the tenant subsequent to the purchase of the
tenant-right, these would, in case of dispute
between him and his landlord, be valued, and the

amount would be regarded as an addition to the price of the Tenant-Right. The tenant having established his claims, and paid the cash balance, and obtained in return his ' Parliamentary Tenant-Right,' would then be irremovable by the landlord except on the terms of repayment to him of the price of his Tenant-Right, which, on the supposition made above, would amount to seven years' purchase of his rental, or 350*l.* It is not proposed to interfere directly with the right of the landlord to raise his rent; but it is proposed to subject his exercise of the right to this check: where the landlord demanded an advance of rent which the tenant declined to pay, the latter might call for the payment of his ' Parliamentary Tenant-Right,' and this, in the supposed case, would be calculated on seven years' purchase of the *increased rent* demanded.

"Such is the proposal ; and it will be seen at once that it involves no principle which is not fully recognized in the (1870) Government Bill. Putting aside the payment of a balance in cash, to be afterwards refunded in the event of a disturbance of occupancy, and which I own seems to be an unnecessary complication of the scheme, it differs from the Government plan mainly in this, that it calls for a settlement of the reciprocal claims of landlords and tenants at once as a basis for the determination of their future relations ; whereas the Government Bill leaves this to be determined by litigation as differences may hereafter arise. Under the ' Parliamentary Tenant-Right ' scheme, every tenant would know his exact position ; *he would see the exact dimensions of the barrier between him and eviction.* Under the Government plan, he only knows that it will be such as a court, proceeding on principles of which he is ignorant, and dealing with disputed facts, may award. What the award in this case is likely to be, he will be unable to form any clear notion of till a considerable number of precedents shall have been established ; and every precedent implies an eviction. It is true that, under the ' Parliamentary Tenant-Right ' plan, the same questions would have to be solved which must be solved under the Government scheme ; but there would be this difference between the two cases, which in practice would amount to a great deal. The former plan contemplates an arrangement between landlord and tenant on the assumption that the tenant is holding on. Under such circumstances neither party would be very anxious to push his pretensions to an extreme. The landlord at the time of settlement is not asked to pay anything, and, if matters proceed harmoniously, may never be asked ; he would also, if the plan took effect in its integrity, most probably be getting an outlay upon his land which would add to the security for his rent.   One may easily conceive in what a different spirit parties would come to a settlement under such circumstances, from that which might be expected where the issue would be to close relations for ever, where one party would be heavily mulcted, and the other, though consoled by a sum of money in hand, would yet be suffering from the embittered feelings which forcible disturbance of possession can scarcely fail to produce.   I have to apologize for the length to which this letter has run ; but the proposal I have undertaken to describe seems to me to deserve public attention.   I have said that it is understood to have the sanction of high authority, and that it has met with unusual favour from the most opposite political parties in Ireland. It has been seen that it involves no principle not recognized in the Government Bill, and, consequently, might be embodied partially or entirely in that Bill by modifications in committee ; and I think I have shown that it contains some substantial merits."[8]

Of the " Longfield Lease " I shall merely say that, like the " Portacarron Lease," it has been tried (in the County Antrim), and has been found to work well.

    [8] *Daily News*, March 13, 1870, and *Vide* Appendix G.

Such are some of the principal proposals for the solution of the " Irish Difficulty " which have now been brought to the front. As it has been my object throughout these pages less to express opinions than to cite facts, I shall content myself with merely directing the attention of my readers to them. I may, however, add, that in my judgment the *minimum* measure of legislation which the Irish tenants are now likely to entertain with favour, must include a scheme for : (1) the exten·sion of the Ulster custom (strictly defined by Act of Parliament) throughout the whole country ; (2) the institution of some procedure for fixing rent which will no longer leave the matter to be solely regulated by the will of the landlord on the one hand, and the necessities of the tenant on the other ; and (3) the adoption of an improved machinery for the working of the Bright clauses, and the amendment of those clauses themselves in such a way as may more effectually tend to the attainment of the end for which they were framed.

More than this the Irish tenants may demand ; less I do not believe they will accept as a final settlement of the Land Question.

VIII.
CONCLUSION.

" I ASK you, my lords," said Earl Grey in 1846, " would an Irish parliament, fairly representing the great mass of the nation, have delayed Catholic emancipation until 1829." [1]

It is not my intention to discuss the subject of " Home Rule " in these pages. But one may well feel impelled, like Lord Grey, to ask, would an Irish parliament, representing the great mass of the nation, have delayed the settlement of the land question until 1880. Let Englishmen be assured that this is a question which the peasantry of Ireland ask themselves over and over again. And it is idle for English statesmen to expect that the Irish people will believe in the superior advantages of an imperial over a domestic parliament, so long as the relation of landlord and tenant is allowed to remain in its present unsatisfactory and disturbing condition.

" The great evil of Ireland," says Mr. Bright, " is

[1] Hansard lxxxiv., 3rd series, 1367.

this, that the Irish people—the Irish nation—are dispossessed from the soil, and what we ought to do is to provide for, and aid in, their restoration to it by all measures of justice." But the Irish people —the Irish nation—think that the English parlia· ment is unable, hesitant, or unwilling, " to provide for, and aid in, their restoration to the soil ;" and assuredly they have received some reason for so thinking. The Irish people assisted their English fellow-citizens in the struggle for parliamentary reform in 1832—but how little did the reformed parliament do for Ireland ?

"For once—for the only time since the union," said Mr. Bright in 1869, "there is a parliament willing to do justice to Ireland ;" [2] and in 1870 Mr. Gladstone admitted that "neglect" was "charge-able upon the parliament elected under the Re-form Bill in respect of the question of Irish land tenure." [3]

The Irish people· feel to-day, as an English Cabinet Minister once declared, that if their country had been "removed 2000 mi es away," that if "she had been a state of the American Republic, justice would have been done her " long ago. [4]

---

[2] Hansard, cxcv., 3rd series, 2016.
[3] Hansard, cxcix., 3rd series, 334.
[4] Hansard, cxcv., 2014.

Is it wise to permit this feeling to exist in the future as it has existed in the past ?

In all her great emergencies Ireland has looked to the south, or to the west, but never to the east.

Is this to be her attitude still ? Is the " union " between Great Britain and Ireland always to continue a union between Great Britain and a colony in Ulster, and nothing more ? Will the progress and loyalty of the north compensate ever for the misery and disaffection of the south, and of the east, and of the west ? It is for the parliament of England now to say. One thing is plain. The tranquillity of the south can only be secured by the adoption of a policy similar to that by which the prosperity of the north was established.

The pains which were taken by Chichester and Davis must, on a far larger scale, and for nobler purposes, be taken by Mr. Gladstone, Mr. Bright, Mr. Forster, and Lord Hartington, to root, not the landlords, but the tenants in the soil of Ireland.

APPENDICES.

Appendix A.

WASTE LANDS.

Extract from the " Report of the Committee on Irish Bogs in 1814," p. 153.

" HAVING pointed out what we conceive to be the main obstacle to the improvement of the bogs—viz. the uncertainty of the boundaries when they pass through extensive bogs, and the right usually vested in the occupiers of adjoining farms, we feel it to be rather the province of the legislature than of our board to devise provisions which can alone remove the impediment. It is also obvious that in the event of future enterprises, either of individuals or associated companies, for the drainage of large tracts of bogs, it will be expedient that the legislature should secure by enactment a free passage under proper regulations through the adjacent estates, so far as may be requisite, for carrying on and completing the main lines of drainage and communication, as otherwise the interested opposition of a neighbouring proprietor might impede and render of no effect the efforts of the improver."

Extract from the evidence of the celebrated Engineer, Mr. Nimmo, given before the Commission on Irish Bogs (1814), p. 154.

" Upon the whole I am so perfectly convinced of the

practicability of converting the whole of the bogs of Ireland I have surveyed into arable land, and that at an expense which need hardly ever exceed the gross value of one year's crop, that I declare myself willing, for a reasonable consideration, to undertake the drainage of any given piece of considerable extent, and the formation of its roads, for the sum of one guinea per acre, which is little more than seven years' purchase of the rent which it would then afford."

APPENDIX B.

THE IRISH LAND QUESTION AND EMIGRATION.

Extracts from Lord Stanley's speech in presenting to the House of Lords his Tenants' Compensation (Ireland) Bill in 1845. (Hansard, 3rd series, vol. lxxxi., p. 211 *et seq.*, June 9, 1845.)

" If the relative circumstances of landlord and tenant were the same in Ireland as they are in England, I do not know that I should be disposed to support any bill to interfere with those relations. But the circumstances of Ireland and England in this respect are so different, that I think a sufficient reason for such interference is proved. In England, though it is certainly true that there are many very large estates, it is also true that there are a large number of only a moderate extent. Property is considerably subdivided throughout the country ; the number of freeholds of moderate extent are large, and the number of very large extent is not, comparatively speaking, so great as in Ireland. . . . Then again, in England the farms generally are of some considerable extent. Sixty or seventy acres is a small holding for one farmer, and it often happens that the farms extend to many hundreds of acres. Here too the tenant-farmer is a class distinct from the agricultural labourer ; for though there are many tenant-farmers who cultivate their land with their own hands, yet the class of tenant-farmers of England are distinct as a class from agricultural labourers ; and lastly, every tenant-farmer on taking a farm in England, and, I believe, in Scotland, looks, as a matter of course, to the landlord to place the farm, before he enters, in tenantable repair ; that is, in regard to the fences, the drains, the dwelling-houses and buildings, and, in short, in regard to all those things which in England are considered as the necessary accompaniments of a farm. But in Ireland the case is not only dissimilar, but exactly the reverse. There the number of the proprietors is small, and their average holdings large ; the farms of the smallest possible dimensions. Your lordships will find, on examining the Report of the Poor Law Commissioners made in 1843, that complaints were made to the commissioners as to the practice of con-solidating farms, and of the hardship of the practice which was growing up of throwing several small farms into one large one ; and upon the question being asked to what extent the farms were raised by this practice of consolidation, it turned out that these large farms amounted to twenty-five, fifteen, and in some cases to no more than ten acres. Farms of fifty, down to twenty statute acres, were looked upon in Ireland as exorbitant holdings—the universal practice being that all buildings, including even the dwelling-house, all fences and drains, which in England are put in repair by the land-lord, are expected to be done by the tenant, and if not they are not done at all. Now imagine the case of any one of your lordships having an estate of 20,000*l.* a year divided into twenty-acre farms, the tenants being tenants-at-will only, and required not only to make good and keep in repair all drains, fences, and out-buildings, but even to build their own dwelling-houses. Could that noble lord be surprised to find that no improvement took place in those farms, and that the dwellings of the tenants were mere hovels ?   Could he be surprised to find on those farms everything neglected and in ruin, the land unproductive, the cultivation defective, and the estate peopled by an idle, dissolute, and disturbed population?   And yet this, with some honourable exceptions, is not a highly coloured picture of the position of a large portion of the tenantry of Ireland.   Then is not this a state of things in which it is for the interest, even of the landlord himself, that we should interfere to give to the tenant some security and encouragement, that if he choose to spend his capital and labour in improvements that increase the value of the property, he should not be turned out of his wretched hovel without compensation for his outlay, whether of money or labour ? . . . It is not space that is wanted in Ireland.   I am not prepared to say that the country is overpopulated. There are in Ireland tracts of waste lands which might be brought into cultivation, and many other tracts which, though now in cultivation, might be made more productive under improved management, and by further expenditure of capital."

(The population of Ireland in 1845 was 8,000,000; it is now 5,000,000

Mr. Bright on Irish Emigration.   Extract from Speech delivered in the House of Commons, April 2, 1849.

" The right hon. gentleman the member for Tamworth spoke about emigration, and I think that he was rather unjust, or at least unwise, in his observations with regard to voluntary emigration.   Things that are done voluntarily are not always done well ; neither are things that are done by the Government ; and I know many cases where Government undertakings have failed as eminently as any that have been attempted by private enterprise.   But it does not appear to me that there is much wisdom in the project of emigration, although I know that hon. gentlemen from Ireland place great faith in it as a remedy. I have endeavoured to ascertain what is the relation of the population to the land in Ireland, and this is what I find. In speaking of the Clifden Union, the inspectors state : ' In conclusion we beg to offer our matured opinion that the resources of the union would, if made available, be amply sufficient for the independent support of its population.'

" Mr. Hamilton, who was examined before the committee of which I am a member, said, speaking of the unions of Donegal and Glenties, ' There is no over-population if those unions, according to their capabilities, were cultivated as the average of English counties, with some skill and capital.' And Mr. Twistleton said, ' I did not speak of a redundant population in reference to land, only to capital. The land of Ireland could maintain double its present population.'

" Then, if that be the case, I am not quite certain that we should be wise in raising sums of money to enable the people to emigrate. The cost of transporting a family to Australia, or even to Canada, is considerable ; and the question is, whether, with the means which it would require to convey them to a distant shore, they might not be more profitably employed at home."

("Collected Speeches of Mr. Bright," popular edition, pp. 172, 173.)

APPENDIX C.

IRISH TRADE AND COMMERCE AND ENGLISH LEGISLATION.

" Until the time of Charles I. Ireland was placed commercially, on all points, on a level with England.

*　　*　　*　　*　　*

" With Charles II., however, legislative prohibitions began.

P

Ireland was a great pasture country, and her chief source of wealth was the importation of her cattle into England. The English landlords complained of the rivalry, and the importation of Irish cattle to England, as well as of salt beef, bacon, butter, and cheese, was absolutely prohibited. By her omission from the amended Navigation Act of 1663 Ireland was at the same time excluded from all direct trade with the British colonies. Her two chief sources of wealth were thus utterly and wilfully annihilated. One chance, however, still remained. The Irish, when forbidden to export their cattle, turned their land into sheepwalks, and it soon appeared that, in spite of the poverty of the people, and the low condition of civilization, a great flourishing woollen trade was likely to arise. Ireland possessed the advantages of an unlimited water supply, of cheap labour and living, and, above all, of the best wool in Europe. Many English, and even foreign manufacturers went over, and in the first years that followed the Revolution there was every probability of her becoming a considerable nation. Once more the selfish policy of English manufacturers prevailed. The export of unmanufactured wool to foreign countries had been already forbidden. The Legislature now interposed, and forbade the export of Irish manufactured wool, not only to England and English dominions, but to every other country. The rising industry was thus completely annihilated. Thousands of manufacturers and of workmen emigrated to the Continent or to America. Whole districts were thrown into a condition of poverty verging upon starvation."—Lecky's reply to Mr. Frances's "English in Ireland in the Eighteenth Century." *Macmillan's Magazine,* January, 1873, pp. 258-9.

APPENDIX D.

LANDLORD LEGISLATION.

Extract from a Speech delivered in the House of Commons, on the 3rd April, 1846, by Daniel O'Connell. (" Collected Speeches," edited by M. H. Cusack, vol. ii. p. 201.)

" Although there had been some murders committed in Ireland that were not directly traceable to evictions from land, yet in sum and substance the whole form and state of society showed it was from evictions from land, from the insecurity of land holdings, from the difficulties arising through the want of land, that we must seek for the great and primary cause of all these crimes. There were some exceptions, he admitted, but he was sorry to say that those exceptions were becoming more numerous. The truth was so, and he did not shrink from stating the truth. The great fault, however, was the land question. The fact was, that that house had done too much for the landlord, and too little for the occupier. What had been the first measure for the benefit of the landlords ? The first statute passed after the Union in favour of the landlords was the Act 56 George III., c. 88, which gave them additional powers to work out ejectments. Up to that time they had not the power to distrain. The statutes of England were not enacted in Ireland towards landlords, but the Act 56 George III., c. 88, gave them powers which were no part of the bargain at the time of the Union. Many parties had taken leases and made contracts without those new powers being in the hands of the landlords. The statute gave them the power of distraining growing crops, keeping them till ripe, saving and selling them when ripe, charging upon the tenant the accumulation of expense. All these powers were first introduced by this statute and conferred upon the Irish landlord. He did not believe there had ever been a more fertile source of murder and outrage than these powers. Thus the source of crime was directly traceable to the legislation of that house ; and it was the imperative duty of that house, and every member in it, immediately, or as speedily as possible, to repeal that Act. Then there came the Act 58 George III., c. 39, for civil bill ejectment. First, the power was given upon the growing crop, enabling the landlord to ruin the tenant, and then there came the further power to the landlord of turning out the tenant from his holding. The Act 1 George IV., c. 41, extended the power of civil bill ejectment ; and the Act 1 George IV., c. 87, enabled the landlords to get security for costs from defendants in ejectments. Then the Act 1 and 2 George IV., c. 31, gave the landlords the right of immediate execution in ejectment ; and the Act 6 and 7 William IV. gave further facilities for civil bill ejectments. All these were additional powers to the landlord. And it was to these statutes that the late Lord Chief Justice Penne-father referred when he said their object was to forward the interests of the landlord."

Extract from a speech of Mr. C. Russell, M.P., delivered in the House of Commons on the 25th June, 1880.

"No such thing as ejectment for non-payment of rent merely is known to the common law, or to the statute law of England. If by the terms of the compact between landlord and tenant there is a clause of re-entry, then upon failure by the tenant to observe the covenants, amongst others payment of rent, the landlord has the right of ejectment. It follows, therefore, that in every case of letting which does not comprise this clause of re-entry the landlord's remedy is to terminate the tenancy by notice.

"The peculiar hardship which the power of ejectment entails in Ireland is this. On the best managed estates there it is usual to leave a half year's rent—called a running gale—in arrear. On well managed estates, where the tenants pay their rents punctually, it is not considered unreasonable that the rent which is due in May should not be paid until the following Christmas. The operation of the exceptional law in Ireland as to ejectment for non-payment of rent is this (let it be marked) :—Suppose that by the 1st of May following the tenant was unable to pay the rent, he would then be a year's rent in arrear ; and by the law of Ireland, which is not the law of England, the tenant would be turned out of his holding by the landlord without any notice to quit whatever, and the only means by which he could live would be taken from him without any compensation. In similar cases in England the landlord must give a year's notice to quit, ending with the year of the tenancy."

APPENDIX E.

THE PORTSMOUTH (ULSTER) CUSTOM.

*　　*　　*　　*　　*

" The agricultural property (for the town property is managed differently in some respects) consists of about 11,00 statute acres, held by farmers whose holdings vary from twenty to 200 acres. The tenure is for whichever lasts longest—a lease for a life or thirty-one years. The landlord has the raw material, on which he has spent nothing. The tenant or his predecessors have alone expended money and energy on it. The landlord's interest is consulted on a re-letting at the expiration of a lease, when from one-eighth to one-fourth is added to Griffith's valuation of the land only— treating Griffith's valuations of the building as the valuation of the tenant's property only. The variations in the valua- tion from one-eighth to one-fourth are decided by the nature of the soil, and by the contiguity of the farm in question to the town of Enniscorthy, which, in spite of the higher rates, increases its value. The tenant's right is to the improvement on the raw material—the house, the farm-buildings, the fences, and the trees planted and registered by him. Therefore, if a tenant wishes to renew a lease on the expiration of an old one, all such improvements are treated as absolutely his own. It is quite possible for a landlord to regret that he could not under this system introduce newer, better, or a more convenient style of building, that he could not carry out for his tenants such reforms as he might deem advantageous and useful ; but, on the other hand, this plan benefits him largely, as it assures an unanswerable security for the contentment and satisfaction of the tenant. At his own convenience, in his own manner, consulting his own fancy, he can execute improvements which, whatever their character, are the result of his own personal wishes, thoughts, and energy. We all know how very far this goes to make a home, its surroundings, and all its associations endeared to us. It has gone very far to make the tenantry of which I write conscious of a just pride themselves, and of the respect of others. This, however, is but the first instalment of success which a system based on this principle obtains. The second— the right of free sale by the tenant of all his own improvements, is even a larger and more important benefit to both landlord and tenant. Let us suppose a tenant wishes to dispose of his holding before the expiration of his lease. By private treaty or by public auction he offers for sale the goodwill or interest of his farm, asking of the incoming tenant or purchaser a price in proportion to his expenditure on improvements, and the length of the unexpired time of the lease, for which he may get from ten to fourteen years' purchase of his annual rent. The tenant thus obtains all the advantage of his own industry and enterprise, and can gauge the worth of all the additions and improvements he has made by the success of his sale and the prices it realizes.

As a rule the outgoing tenant nominates the incoming one. To prevent fraud the landlord has the right of veto, but it is hardly necessary to add, that such a right would be exercised only for very rare and special reasons ; for it is obvious that this system, by procuring a ready successor to a vacant farm, signifies the new man's approval of what he finds upon it, and his power to satisfy the outgoing man, who is unwilling or unable to continue in the place."   *   *   *
—Lord Lymington in *The Nineteenth Century*, Oct. 1, 1880.

Appendix F.

THE PORTACARRON LEASE (PRINCIPAL PROVISIONS).

*   *   *   *   *

" Provided always and it is hereby agreed that for the purpose of enabling the lessor his heirs and assigns or the lessee his executors administrators and assigns to claim from time to time as hereinafter mentioned an increase or decrease of the said reserved rent according to the prices of the ten following articles wheat oats barley potatoes hay wool beef mutton pork and butter the average prices for the ten years ending on the thirty-first December one thousand eight hundred and seventy-one of those ten articles shall be taken and admitted to have been as set forth in the schedule hereon endorsed and that the said reserved rent of nine pounds two shillings is at the time of the execution hereof of the value of the weights and decimal parts of such weights in said schedule stated of wheat oats barley potatoes hay wool beef mutton pork and butter respectively which would have been purchased at the prices aforesaid in case one-tenth part of such rent had been invested in the purchase of wheat one-tenth part thereof in the purchase of oats one-tenth part thereof in the purchase of barley one-tenth part thereof in the purchase of potatoes one-tenth part thereof in the purchase of hay one-tenth part thereof in the purchase of wool one-tenth part thereof in the purchase of beef one-tenth part thereof in the purchase of mutton one-tenth part thereof in the purchase of pork and one-tenth part thereof in the purchase of butter   And it shall be lawful for the lessor his heirs and assigns or for the lessee his executors administrators and assigns to signify the one to the other by notice in writing four months next after the expiration of ten years to be computed from the thirty-first day of December next preceding the date hereof and in like manner at any time by like notice four months next after the expiration of any and every subsequent period of ten years such period to be computed each from the termination of the preceding period during the continuance of the said term the desire of such lessor his heirs or assigns or of such lessee his executors administrators or assigns to have the average prices of the said ten articles for the ten years next preceding ascertained in order that the annual rent payable under this demise at the said period may be increased or diminished for the ensuing ten years in proportion to such average prices and for that purpose to nominate and appoint two persons one to be chosen by the lessor his heirs or assigns and one to be chosen by the lessee his executors administrators or assigns to be arbitrators for ascertaining the same accordingly (such arbitrators to have power to appoint an umpire) the decision of the arbitrators if they agree or if they do not agree of the umpire to be binding on the lessor his heirs or assigns and on the lessee his executors administrators and assigns and for such arbitrators or umpire to ascertain from the "Dublin Gazette" or from other authentic and reliable sources the prices of said ten articles as aforesaid and if it shall appear that the average prices of all said articles together in such proportions as aforesaid for such preceding period of ten years is more or less by one-tenth than the average prices hereof set forth in the said schedule then and in such case the amount of the annual rent to be paid out of said lands to the lessor his heirs and assigns by the lessee his executors administrators and assigns shall be increased or diminished in such manner and to such extent that the amount of such annual rent payable for and during the next ensuing ten years shall bear the like proportion to the amount of the annual rent reserved and made payable out of the said premises by this demise as the average prices of said ten articles as ascertained at the time of such notice shall bear to the average prices thereof as stated in said schedule and the said arbitrators or umpire shall thereupon by writing to be signed by such arbitrators or umpire endorsed on these presents or by separate label attached hereto set forth the said average prices so ascertained and the amount of such revised or new annual rent to be payable for the then next period of ten years and such annual rent shall be paid to the lessor his heirs and assigns by the lessee his executors administrators and assigns for the next period of ten years and until such revised or new annual rent shall afterwards upon a like notice and at like period be again valued and ascertained. And it shall be lawful for the lessor his heirs and assigns or for the lessee his executors administrators and assigns to give such notice from time to time four months next after the expiration of every period of ten years during the continuance of this demise in such and the like manner as hereby agreed on with respect to the said first notice and the costs charges and expenses of every such notice of varying revising and ascertaining the amount of such annual rent shall be defrayed by the person or persons requiring the same and any such revised or new annual rent shall during the period aforesaid stand in the place of the rent hereby reserved and shall be paid and recoverable and charged and chargeable upon said premises in like manner as said reserved rent and subject to the same regulations.

Provided always that the said reserved rent shall continue to be used as the standard by reference to which together with the said original prices of the said ten articles the rent is to be from time to time varied as aforesaid.

Provided always that the person serving any such notice as aforesaid shall state therein and thereby appoint his arbitrator and the person served with any such notice shall within twenty days after being served therewith serve in reply upon the person serving such notice a memorandum in writing naming and appointing the arbitrator of the person served with such notice and in all other respects such arbitrators umpire and arbitration shall be subject to and conducted according to the provisions respecting arbitration in that behalf contained in the Common Law Procedure Act 1856 or any then subsisting statutory modification thereof.

Provided always that at any time within four months next after the expiration of any period of ten years as aforesaid but not oftener or after periods of shorter duration than ten years the lessor his heirs or assigns and lessee his executors administrators or assigns may without the appointment or action of arbitrators as hereinbefore provided mutually agree to any increase or decrease of rent for the decennial period then entered upon and the rent so mutually agreed upon shall be endorsed upon these presents or by separate label attached hereto and such endorsement shall be duly authenticated by the signatures respectively of the lessor his heirs or assigns and the lessee his executors administrators or assigns and of a witness or of witnesses and the amount of such mutually agreed upon rent shall be payable and paid during the decennial period within which it was so mutually agreed upon as if said rent had been ascertained by arbitration as hereinbefore provided and such mutually agreed upon rent shall continue to be payable and paid until an increased or decreased rent shall be mutually agreed upon or ascertained by arbitration as hereinbefore provided."

*   *   *   *   *

APPENDIX G.

THE LONGFIELD LEASE (PRINCIPAL PROVISIONS).

*　　　*　　　*　　　*　　　*

" And it is hereby agreed between the parties hereto that it shall be lawful for the said tenant, his executors, administrators, or assigns, at any time between the first day of November, 1886, and the first day of May, 1887, to serve a notice on the said landlord, which notice shall be to the following effect : that is to say, that the tenant desires to have the term of his lease extended for the further term of ten years from the expiration of his then existing interest, at a yearly rent to be named in such notice, for such extended term, and the effect of such notice shall be that if the landlord shall assent thereto the tenant shall hold the premises for the additional term of ten years, at the yearly rent named therein, payable at the times hereinbefore mentioned, and subject to all the covenants, clauses, and conditions herein contained, and the landlord shall be bound to grant a new lease to the tenant on the terms aforesaid, and the tenant shall execute a counterpart thereof, and shall pay to the landlord for the costs of such lease and counterpart the sum of 3*l.* sterling, together with the amount of any stamp duty to which such lease and counterpart shall be liable ; and if the landlord shall refuse to consent to the terms of such notice, the tenant shall surrender the premises on the first day of November next following the date thereof, and shall receive from the landlord a sum equal to seven times the amount of the rent offered in the said notice, and such sum shall be a charge on the premises and shall bear interest at the rate of 5*l.* per cent. per annum until paid off, such interest to be payable on the first day of May, and the first day of November in each year.

And it is hereby further agreed between the parties hereto that it shall be lawful for the landlord, at any time between the first day of November, 1886, and the first day of May,

1887, to serve a notice on the tenant—stating that he is willing to extend the term of the tenant's lease for the further term of ten years from the expiration of his then existing interest, at a yearly rent to be named in such notice for such extended term ; and the effect of such notice shall be that if the tenant shall assent thereto the tenant shall hold the premises for the additional term of ten years, at the yearly rent named therein, payable at the times hereinbefore mentioned, and subject to all the covenants, clauses, and conditions herein contained ; and the landlord shall be bound to grant a new lease to the tenant on the terms aforesaid, and the tenant shall execute a counterpart thereof, and shall pay to the landlord for the cost of such lease and counterpart the sum of 3*l.* sterling, together with the amount of any stamp duty to which such lease and counterpart shall be liable, and if the tenant shall refuse to consent to the terms of such notice he shall surrender the premises on the first day of November next following the date thereof, and shall receive from the landlord a sum equal to seven times the amount of the yearly rent demanded by the said notice, and such sum shall be a charge upon the premises, and shall bear interest at the rate of 5*l.* per cent. per annum, until paid off, such interest to be payable on the first day of May and the first day of November in each year ; provided also that if neither the landlord nor the tenant shall serve such notice as aforesaid within the respective periods for that purpose hereinbefore specified, in that case the tenant shall hold the premises subject to the same rent, conditions, and covenants, for an additional term of ten years, with the same rights and liabilities as if he had served a notice to that effect, and the landlord had assented to the same.

And it is hereby agreed that all new leases to be granted within two hundred years from the commencement of the term hereby created for the extension of the terms, according to the notices served under the provisions aforesaid, shall contain similar clauses for further extensions by means of notices served a due time before its termination—it being he intent of this indenture that the tenant shall have an interest in the premises renewable for two hundred years, subject to a re-adjustment of the rent at the expiration of every ten years, or shall be entitled to compensation at the rate of rent which has been offered by the tenant or demanded by the landlord, as the case may be ; provided that upon resuming possession of the premises the landlord shall, at the expiration of the said period of two hundred years, pay o the tenant a sum equal to seven times the rent at which the premises shall then be held."

* * * * *

APPENDIX H.

INDUSTRY OF THE IRISH PEASANTRY.

"So far from being uniformly inactive and idle, the peasantry of Ireland have considerable anxiety to procure employment." (Report of Select Committee of House of Commons, on the condition of the labouring poor of Ireland in 1823, p. 6.)

APPENDIX I.

THE SYSTEM OF TENANCIES-AT-WILL.

" What is the spectacle presented to us by Ireland ? It is that of millions of persons whose only dependence and whose chief occupation is agriculture—for the most part cultivating their lands—that is, sinking their past, their present, and their future upon yearly tenancies. What is a yearly tenancy ? Why, it is an impossible tenure—a tenure which, if its terms were to be literally interpreted [and its terms are literally interpreted in Ireland], no Christian man would offer, and none but a madman would accept." (Lord Dufferin, as quoted in Mr. Arthur Arnold's " Free Land," p. 352.)

NOTE.

THE Land Act of 1870 deals substantially with four topics ; (1) the Ulster Custom ; (2) the usages resembling that custom, existing outside Ulster ; (3) cases of tenancies not subject to the Ulster or any analogous Custom ; and (4) the development of a Peasant proprietary.

1. The Act provides that the Ulster Tenant Right Custom shall be converted into law. It had often been contended before the discussions on the Land Act, that the Ulster Custom was too vague and uncertain to be legalized. The principle on which Mr. Gladstone proceeded to deal with the subject is best expressed in his own language. " We do not attempt to modify the Custom. We do not inquire into its varieties (it is well known to vary within certain limits). We do not attempt to improve it, or to qualify it. We leave it to be examined as a matter of fact, and when it shall have been so ascertained, the judge will have nothing to do but to enforce it." Advantage was

taken of some inaccurate phraseology in the Act to obstruct the legalization of the Custom. But a short statute subsequently passed cured this technical defect, and the intentions of the legislature, as expressed by Mr. Gladstone, have since been carried out without any difficulty.

2. The Act conferred the force of law on all usages outside Ulster analogous to the Ulster Custom.

Power was given to the landlords to extinguish the Ulster Custom and similar usages. They were enabled to purchase the right from the tenant if the latter were willing to sell.

3. In the cases of tenancies unprotected by the Ulster Custom, or any analogous usage the Act created two rights previously unknown to the law for the benefit of the tenant. (A) It conferred on the tenant from " year to year " a right to "compensation for disturbance " by eviction. Where the eviction was for non-payment of rent the right to compensation for "disturbance" could not be acquired, except in the case of small holdings subject to an exorbitant rent. The right was restricted, in the case of tenancies existing at the date of the Act, to holdings valued for the purposes of the Irish poor laws at or under 100*l.* a year, and it was limited in all cases by provisions as to the amount to be awarded. The smaller the

holding, the more the tenant was considered to need the protection afforded by this section. If his holding did not exceed in value 10*l.* a year, according to the poor-law valuation, he might claim, as compensation, an amount equal to seven years' rent. This was the *maximum*. If the farm was valued for poor-law purposes at a sum exceeding 100*l.* a year, his compensation could not exceed a year's rent, and in no case could any tenant claim as compensation for eviction a larger sum than 250*l.* Moreover, the County Court Judge was directed to inquire into the facts and circumstances of each claim, and any default or unreasonable conduct of the tenant might lead to the disallowance of part or all of his claim to compensation for disturbance.

(B) The second kind of right created for the benefit of the tenant by the Land Act was the right to " compensation for improvements" effected by him or his predecessors in title. Numerous provisions were introduced to limit and restrict within equitable bounds the enjoyment of this right. It is unnecessary and it would be tedious to the reader to set them forth in detail. The broad rule adopted was that no improvements save those which were suitable to the holding, and added to the letting value of the land could confer the right to this compensation.

4. The fourth object of the Act—the development of a Peasant proprietary—was sought by the Bright clauses, which have been fully dealt with in the text.

As Mr. Gladstone has recently said that the Compensation for Disturbance provided by the Act was "by much its most important feature," I think it right to set out in full the sections by which this right was created and regulated.

" Where the tenant of any holding held by him under a tenancy created after the passing of this Act, is not entitled to compensation under sections one and two of this Act, or either of such sections,[1] or if entitled does not seek compensation under said sections or either of them, and is disturbed in his holding by the act of the landlord, he shall be entitled to such compensation for the loss which the court shall find to be sustained by him by reason of quitting his holding, to be paid by the landlord as the court may think just, so that the sum awarded does not exceed the scale following ; that is to say,

" In the case of holdings valued under the Acts relating to the valuation of rateable property in Ireland at an annual value of—

___

[1] Secs. 1 and 2 referred to the Ulster Custom and analogous usages.

(1.) 10*l.* and under, a sum which shall in no case exceed seven years' rent ;

(2.) Above 10*l.* and not exceeding 30*l.*, a sum which shall in no case exceed five years' rent ;

(3.) Above 30*l.* and not exceeding 40*l.*, a sum which shall in no case exceed four years' rent ;

(4.) Above 40*l.* and not exceeding 50*l.*, a sum which shall in no case exceed three years' rent ;

(5.) Above 50*l.* and not exceeding 100*l.*, a sum which shall in no case exceed two years' rent ;

(6.) Above 100*l.*, a sum which shall in no case exceed one year's rent ;

" But in no case shall the compensation exceed the sum of 250*l.*

" Any tenant in a higher class of the scale, may, at his option, claim compensation under a lower class, provided such compensation shall not exceed the sum to which he would be entitled under such lower class on the assumption that the annual value of his holding is reduced to the sum (or where two sums are mentioned, the highest sum) stated in such lower class, and that his rent is proportionately reduced.

" Provided that no tenant of a holding valued at a

yearly sum exceeding 10*l.*, and claiming under this section more than four years' rent, and no tenant of a holding valued at a yearly sum not exceeding 10*l.*, and claiming as aforesaid, more than five years' rent, shall be entitled to make a separate or additional claim for improvements other than permanent buildings and reclamation of waste land.

" Provided that—

(1.) out of any moneys payable to the tenant under this section all sums due to the landlord from the tenant or his predecessors in title in respect of rent, or in respect of any deterioration of a holding arising from non-observance on the part of the tenant of any express or implied covenant or agreement, may be deducted by the landlord, and also any taxes payable by the tenant due in respect of the holding, and not recoverable by him from the landlord :

(2.) A tenant of a holding who at any time after the passing of this Act subdivides such holding, or sublets the same or any part thereof without the consent of the landlord in writing, or, after he has been prohibited in writing by the landlord or his agent from so doing, lets the same or any part thereof in conacre, save for the purpose of being solely used and which shall be solely used for the growing of potatoes or other green crops, the land being properly manured, shall not, nor shall any sub-tenant of or under any such tenant as last aforesaid, be entitled to any compensation under this section :

(3.) A tenant of a holding under a lease made after the passing of this Act, and granted for a term certain of not less than thirty-one years, shall not be entitled to any compensation under this section, but he may claim compensation under section four of this Act.

"The tenant of any holding valued under the Acts relating to the valuation of rateable property in Ireland at an annual value of not more than one hundred pounds, and held by him under a tenancy from year to year existing at the time of the passing of this Act, shall, if disturbed by the act of his immediate landlord, be entitled to compensation under and subject to the provisions of this section.

"Any contract made by a tenant by virtue of which he is deprived of his right to make any claim which he would otherwise be entitled to make under this section shall, so far as relates to such claim, be void, both at law and in equity ; this provision shall be subject to the enactment contained in the section of this Act relating to the partial exemption of certain tenancies, and remain in force for twenty years from the first day of January, one thousand eight hundred and seventy-one, and no longer, unless Parliament shall otherwise determine." (33 and 34 Vic., c. 46, Sec. 3.)

"For the purposes of this Act ejectment for non-payment of rent, or for breach of any condition against assignment, sub-letting, bankruptcy, or insolvency, shall not be deemed disturbance of the tenant by act of the landlord ; and for the purposes of this Act a person who is ejected for non-payment of rent or for breach of any such condition as aforesaid, and is not disturbed by the act of the landlord within the meaning of this Act, shall stand in the same position in all re-spects as if he were quitting his holding volun-tarily ; provided that in the case of a person claiming compensation on the determination by ejectment for non-payment of rent of a tenancy existing at the time of the passing of this Act, and continuing to exist without alteration of rent up to the time of such determination, the Court may, if it think fit, treat such ejectment as a disturbance if the arrear of rent in respect of which it is brought did not wholly accrue within the three previous years, and if any earlier arrear remained due from the tenant at the time of commencing the ejectment, or if in case of any such tenancy of a holding held at an annual rent not exceeding fifteen pounds, the Court shall certify that the non-payment of rent causing the eviction has arisen from the rent being an exorbitant rent ; provided that no tenant who shall have given notice of surrender, and afterwards refuse to give up possession in pursuance of such notice, shall be entitled to any compensation under section three of this Act, though evicted by the landlord in a suit founded on such notice." (33 and 34 Vic., c. 46, Sec. 9.)

INDEX.

R

main features of, 167, *et seq ;*
Judge Longfield on, 168; how
preserved, 167; results of, 173, *et
seq.*
Uncertainty of tenure, *vide* Tenure.
Spencer on, 13, *et seq.* ; Dobbs
on, 16, *et seq.*

WASTE Lands, Mr. Brownlow's
bill on, 35 ; Marquis of Downshire on, 36; Mr. Grattan on,
38; Mr. Spring Rice on, 39;
Mr. Lynch's bill in 1837, 66 ;
practical legislation in 1842, 66 ;
Mr. McCarthy on, 67.

A Catalogue of American and Foreign Books Published or Imported by MESSRS. SAMPSON LOW & CO. *can be had on application.*

Crown Buildings, 188, *Fleet Street, London,*
April, 1880.

A Selection from the List of Books

PUBLISHED BY

SAMPSON LOW, MARSTON, SEARLE, & RIVINGTON.

ALPHABETICAL LIST.

A CLASSIFIED *Educational Catalogue of Works* published in Great Britain. Demy 8vo, cloth extra. Second Edition, revised and corrected to Christmas, 1879, 5*s.*

About (Edmond). See "The Story of an Honest Man."

About Some Fellows. By an ETON BOY, Author of "A Day of my Life." Cloth limp, square 16mo, 2*s.* 6*d.*

Adventures of Captain Mago. A Phœnician's Explorations 1000 years B.C. By LEON CAHUN. Numerous Illustrations. Crown 8vo, cloth extra, gilt edges, 7*s.* 6*d.* ; plainer binding, 5*s.*

Adventures of a Young Naturalist. By LUCIEN BIART, with 117 beautiful Illustrations on Wood. Edited and adapted by PARKER GILLMORE. Post 8vo, cloth extra, gilt edges, New Edition, 7*s.* 6*d.*

Afghan Knife (The). A Novel. By ROBERT ARMITAGE STERNDALE, Author of "Seonee." Small post 8vo, cloth extra, 6*s.*

Afghanistan and the Afghans. Being a Brief Review of the History of the Country, and Account of its People. By H. W. BELLEW, C.S.I. Crown 8vo, cloth extra, 6*s.*

Alcott (Louisa M.) Jimmy's Cruise in the "Pinafore." With 9 Illustrations. Second Edition. Small post 8vo, cloth gilt, 3*s.* 6*d.*

——— *Aunt Jo's Scrap-Bag.* Square 16mo, 2*s.* 6*d.* (Rose Library, 1*s.*)

——— *Little Men : Life at Plumfield with Jo's Boys.* Small post 8vo, cloth, gilt edges, 3*s.* 6*d.* (Rose Library, Double vol. 2*s.*)

——— *Little Women.* 1 vol., cloth, gilt edges, 3*s.* 6*d.* (Rose Library, 2 vols., 1*s.* each.)

A

Alcott (Louisa M.) Old-Fashioned Girl. Best Edition, small
post 8vo, cloth extra, gilt edges, 3*s.* 6*d.* (Rose Library, 2*s.*)

—— *Work and Beginning Again.* A Story of Experience.
Experience. 1 vol., small post 8vo, cloth extra, 6*s.* Several Illustrations. (Rose Library, 2 vols., 1*s.* each.)

—— *Shawl Straps.* Small post 8vo, cloth extra, gilt, 3*s.* 6*d.*

—— *Eight Cousins; or, the Aunt Hill.* Small post 8vo,
with Illustrations, 3*s.* 6*d.*

—— *The Rose in Bloom.* Small post 8vo, cloth extra,
3*s.* 6*d.*

—— *Silver Pitchers.* Small post 8vo, cloth extra, 3*s.* 6*d.*

—— *Under the Lilacs.* Small post 8vo, cloth extra, 5*s.*

—— *Jack and Jill.* Small post 8vo, cloth extra, 5*s.*
"Miss Alcott's stories are thoroughly healthy, full of racy fun and humour . . . .
exceedingly entertaining . . . . We can recommend the 'Eight Cousins.'"—
Athenæum.

Alpine Ascents and Adventures; or, Rock and Snow Sketches.
By H. SCHÜTZ WILSON, of the Alpine Club. With Illustrations by
WHYMPER and MARCUS STONE. Crown 8vo, 10*s.* 6*d.* 2nd Edition.

Andersen (Hans Christian) Fairy Tales. With Illustrations in
Colours by E. V. B. Royal 4to, cloth, 25*s.*

Animals Painted by Themselves. Adapted from the French of
Balzac, Georges Sands, &c., with 200 Illustrations by GRANDVILLE.
8vo, cloth extra, gilt, 10*s.* 6*d.*

Art Education. See "Illustrated Text Books."

Art in the Mountains: The Story of the Passion Play. By
HENRY BLACKBURN, Author of "Artists and Arabs," "Breton
Folk," &c. With numerous Illustrations, and an Appendix for
Travellers, giving the Expenses of the Journey, Cost of Living, Routes
from England, &c., Map, and Programme for 1880. 4to, cloth, 10*s.* 6*d.*
"Of the many previous accounts of the play, none, we are disposed to think,
recalls that edifying and impressive spectacle with the same clearness and
vividness as Mr. Blackburn's volume."—*Guardian.*
"He writes in excellent taste, and is interesting from the first page to the
last."—*Saturday Review.*

Art of Reading Aloud (The) in Pulpit, Lecture Room, or Private
Reunions. By G. VANDENHOFF, M.A. Crown 8vo, cloth extra, 6*s.*

Art Treasures in the South Kensington Museum. Published,
with the sanction of the Science and Art Department, in Monthly
Parts, each containing 8 Plates, price 1*s.* In this series are included
representations of Decorative Art of all countries and all times from
objects in the South Kensington Museum, under the following classes:—
Sculpture: Works in Marble, Ivory, and Terra-Cotta.
Bronzes: Statuettes, Medallions, Plaques, Coins.
Decorative Painting and Mosaic.

Decorative Furniture and Carved Wood-Work.
Ecclesiastical Metal-Work.
Gold and Silversmiths' Work and Jewellery.
Limoges and Oriental Enamels.
Pottery of all Countries.
Glass: Oriental, Venetian, and German.
Ornamental Iron-Work : Cutlery.
Textile Fabrics : Embroidery and Lace.
Decorative Bookbinding.
Original Designs for Works of Decorative Art.
Views of the Courts and Galleries of the Museum.
Architectural Decorations of the Museum.
The Plates are carefully printed in atlas 8vo (13 in. by 9 in.), on thick ivory-tinted paper ; and are included in a stout wrapper, ornamented with a drawing from " The Genoa Doorway " recently acquired by the Museum.

Asiatic Turkey: being a Narrative of a Journey from Bombay to the Bosphorus. By GRATTAN GEARY, Editor of the *Times of India*. 2 vols., crown 8vo, cloth extra, with many Illustrations, and a Route Map, 28*s*.

Australian Abroad (The). Branches from the Main Routes Round the World. Comprising the Author's Route through Japan, China, Cochin-China, Malasia, Sunda, Java, Torres Straits, Northern Australia, New South Wales, South Australia, and New Zealand. By JAMES HINGSTON ("J. H." of the *Melbourne Argus*). With Maps and numerous Illustrations from Photographs. 2 vols., 8vo, 14*s*. each.

Autobiography of Sir G. Gilbert Scott, R.A., F.S.A., &c. Edited by his Son, G. GILBERT SCOTT. With an Introduction by the DEAN OF CHICHESTER, and a Funeral Sermon, preached in Westminster Abbey, by the DEAN OF WESTMINSTER. Also, Portrait on steel from the portrait of the Author by G. RICHMOND, R.A. 1 vol., demy 8vo, cloth extra, 18*s*.

*B*AKER *(Lieut.-Gen. Valentine, Pasha). See* "War in Bulgaria."

THE BAYARD SERIES,

Edited by the late J. HAIN FRISWELL.

Comprising Pleasure Books of Literature produced in the Choicest Style as Companionable Volumes at Home and Abroad.

"We can hardly imagine better books for boys to read or for men to ponder over."—*Times.*
Price 2s. 6d. each Volume, complete in itself, flexible cloth extra, gilt edges, with silk Headbands and Registers.

The Story of the Chevalier Bayard. By M. DE BERVILLE.
De Joinville's St. Louis, King of France.

The Bayard Series (continued) :—

The Essays of Abraham Cowley, including all his Prose Works.

Abdallah ; or the Four Leaves. By EDOUARD LABOULLAYE.

Table-Talk and Opinions of Napoleon Buonaparte.

Vathek : An Oriental Romance. By WILLIAM BECKFORD.

The King and the Commons. A Selection of Cavalier and Puritan Songs. Edited by Prof. MORLEY.

Words of Wellington : Maxims and Opinions of the Great Duke.

Dr. Johnson's Rasselas, Prince of Abyssinia. With Notes.

Hazlitt's Round Table. With Biographical Introduction.

The Religio Medici, Hydriotaphia, and the Letter to a Friend. By Sir THOMAS BROWNE, Knt.

Ballad Poetry of the Affections. By ROBERT BUCHANAN.

Coleridge's Christabel, and other Imaginative Poems. With Preface by ALGERNON C. SWINBURNE.

Lord Chesterfield's Letters, Sentences, and Maxims. With Introduction by the Editor, and Essay on Chesterfield by M. DE STE.-BEUVE, of the French Academy.

Essays in Mosaic. By THOS. BALLANTYNE.

My Uncle Toby ; his Story and his Friends. Edited by P. FITZGERALD.

Reflections ; or, Moral Sentences and Maxims of the Duke de la Rochefoucauld.

Socrates : Memoirs for English Readers from Xenophon's Memo-rabilia. By EDW. LEVIEN.

Prince Albert's Golden Precepts.

A Case containing 12 Volumes, price 31s. 6d. ; or the Case separately, price 3s. 6d.

Beauty and the Beast. An Old Tale retold, with Pictures by E. V. B. 4to, cloth extra. 10 Illustrations in Colours. 12s. 6d.

Beumers' German Copybooks. In six gradations at 4d. each.

Biart (Lucien). See "Adventures of a Young Naturalist," "My Rambles in the New World," "The Two Friends," "Involuntary Voyage."

Bickersteth's Hymnal Companion to Book of Common Prayer
may be had in various styles and bindings from 1*d.* to 21*s.* *Price*
List and Prospectus will be forwarded on application.

Bickersteth (Rev. E. H., M.A.) The Reef and other Parables.
1 vol., square 8vo, with numerous very beautiful Engravings, 2*s.* 6*d.*

—— *The Clergyman in his Home.* Small post 8vo, 1*s.*

—— *The Master's Home-Call; or, Brief Memorials of*
Alice Frances Bickersteth. 20th Thousand. 32mo, cloth gilt, 1*s.*

—— *The Master's Will.* A Funeral Sermon preached
on the Death of Mrs. S. Gurney Buxton. Sewn, 6*d.* ; cloth gilt, 1*s.*

—— *The Shadow of the Rock.* A Selection of Religious
Poetry. 18mo, cloth extra, 2*s.* 6*d.*

—— *The Shadowed Home and the Light Beyond.* 7th
Edition, crown 8vo, cloth extra, 5*s.*

Bida. The Authorized Version of the Four Gospels, with the
whole of the magnificent Etchings on Steel, after drawings by M.
BIDA, in 4 vols., appropriately bound in cloth extra, price 3*l.* 3*s.* each.
Also the four volumes in two, bound in the best morocco, by Suttaby,
extra gilt edges, 18*l.* 18*s.*, half-morocco, 12*l.* 12*s.*

"Bida's Illustrations of the Gospels of St. Matthew and St. John have already
received here and elsewhere a full recognition of their great merits."—*Times.*

Biographies of the Great Artists, Illustrated. This Series is
issued in the form of Handbooks. Each is a Monograph of a Great
Artist, and contains Portraits of the Masters, and as many examples
of their art as can be readily procured. They are Illustrated with from
16 to 20 Full-page Engravings. Cloth, large crown 8vo, 3*s.* 6*d.* per
Volume.

Titian.	**Rubens.**	**Tintoret and Veronese.**
Rembrandt.	**Leonardo.**	**Hogarth.**
Raphael.	**Turner.**	**Michelangelo.**
Van Dyck and Hals.	**The Little Masters.**	**Reynolds.**
Holbein.	**Delaroche & Vernet.**	**Gainsborough.**
	Figure Painters of Holland.	

"A deserving Series, based upon recent German publications."—*Edinburgh
Review.*
"Most thoroughly and tastefully edited."—*Spectator.*

Black (Wm.) Three Feathers. Small post 8vo, cloth extra, 6*s.*

—— *Lady Silverdale's Sweetheart, and other Stories.* 1 vol.,
small post 8vo, 6*s.*

—— *Kilmeny: a Novel.* Small post 8vo, cloth, 6*s.*

—— *In Silk Attire.* 3rd Edition, small post 8vo, 6*s.*

—— *A Daughter of Heth.* 11th Edition, small post 8vo, 6*s.*

—— *Sunrise.* 15 Monthly Parts, 1*s.* each.

Blackmore (R. D.) Lorna Doone. 10th Edition, cr. 8vo, 6s.

—— — *Alice Lorraine.* 1 vol., small post 8vo, 6th Edition, 6s.

——·— *Clara Vaughan.* Revised Edition, 6s.

——··—— *Cradock Nowell.* New Edition, 6s.

—— — *Cripps the Carrier.* 3rd Edition, small post 8vo, 6s.

———— *Mary Anerley.* 3 vols., 31s. 6d.

———— *Erema ; or, My Father's Sin.* With 12 Illustrations, small post 8vo, 6s.

Blossoms from the King's Garden : Sermons for Children. By the Rev. C. BOSANQUET. 2nd Edition, small post 8vo, cloth extra, 6s.

Blue Banner (The) ; or, The Adventures of a Mussulman, a Christian, and a Pagan, in the time of the Crusades and Mongol Conquest. Translated from the French of LEON CAHUN. With Seventy-six Wood Engravings. Imperial 16mo, cloth, gilt edges, 7s. 6d. ; plainer binding, 5s.

Boy's Froissart (The). 7s. 6d. *See "Froissart."*

Brave Janet : A Story for Girls. By ALICE LEE. With Frontispiece by M. ELLEN EDWARDS. Square 8vo, cloth extra, 3s. 6d.

Brave Men in Action. By S. J. MACKENNA. Crown 8vo, 480 pp., cloth, 10s. 6d.

Brazil : the Amazons, and the Coast. By HERBERT H. SMITH. With 115 Full-page and other Illustrations. Demy 8vo, 650 pp., 21s.

Brazil and the Brazilians. By J. C. FLETCHER and D. P. KIDDER. 9th Edition, Illustrated, 8vo, 21s.

Breton Folk : An Artistic Tour in Brittany. By HENRY BLACKBURN, Author of " Artists and Arabs," " Normandy Picturesque," &c. With 171 Illustrations by RANDOLPH CALDECOTT. Imperial 8vo, cloth extra, gilt edges, 21s.

British Goblins : Welsh Folk-Lore, Fairy Mythology, Legends, and Traditions. By WIRT SYKES, United States Consul for Wales. With Illustrations by J. H. THOMAS. This account of the Fairy Mythology and Folk-Lore of his Principality is, by permission, dedicated to H.R.H. the Prince of Wales. Second Edition. 8vo, 18s.

British Philosophers.

Buckle (Henry Thomas) The Life and Writings of. By ALFRED HENRY HUTH. With Portrait. 2 vols., demy 8vo.

Burnaby (Capt.) See "On Horseback."

Burnham Beeches (Heath, F. G.). With numerous Illustrations and a Map. Crown 8vo, cloth, gilt edges, 3s. 6d. Second Edition.

"Writing with even more than his usual brilliancy, Mr. HEATH here gives the public an interesting monograph of the splendid old trees. . . . This charming little work."—*Globe.*

Butler (*W. F.*) *The Great Lone Land; an Account of the Red* River Expedition, 1869-70. With Illustrations and Map. Fifth and Cheaper Edition, crown 8vo, cloth extra, 7s. 6d.

—————— *The Wild North Land; the Story of a Winter Journey* with Dogs across Northern North America. Demy 8vo, cloth, with numerous Woodcuts and a Map, 4th Edition, 18s. Cr. 8vo, 7s. 6d.

—————— *Akim-foo : the History of a Failure.* Demy 8vo, cloth, 2nd Edition, 16s. Also, in crown 8vo, 7s. 6d.

CADOGAN (*Lady A.*) *Illustrated Games of Patience.* Twenty-four Diagrams in Colours, with Descriptive Text. Foolscap 4to, cloth extra, gilt edges, 3rd Edition, 12s. 6d.

Caldecott (*R.*). *See* " Breton Folk."

Carbon Process (*A Manual of*). *See* LIESEGANG.

Ceramic Art. See JACQUEMART.

Changed Cross (*The*), and other Religious Poems. 16mo, 2s. 6d.

Chant Book Companion to the Book of Common Prayer. Consisting of upwards of 550 Chants for the Daily Psalms and for the Canticles ; also Kyrie Eleisons, and Music for the Hymns in Holy Communion, &c. Compiled and Arranged under the Musical Editorship of C. J. VINCENT, Mus. Bac. Crown 8vo, 2s. 6d. ; Organist's Edition, fcap. 4to, 5s.

Of various Editions of HYMNAL COMPANION, *Lists will be forwarded on application.*

Child of the Cavern (*The*) *; or, Strange Doings Underground.* By JULES VERNE. Translated by W. H. G. KINGSTON. Numerous Illustrations. Sq. cr. 8vo, gilt edges, 7s. 6d. ; cl., plain edges, 5s.

Child's Play, with 16 Coloured Drawings by E. V. B. Printed on thick paper, with tints, 7s. 6d.

—————— *New.* By E. V. B. Similar to the above. *See* New.

Children's Lives and How to Preserve Them ; or, The Nursery Handbook. By W. LOMAS, M.D. Crown 8vo, cloth, 5s.

Children's Magazine. Illustrated. *See* St. Nicholas.

Choice Editions of Choice Books. 2s. 6d. each, Illustrated by C. W. COPE, R.A., T. CRESWICK, R.A., E. DUNCAN, BIRKET FOSTER, J. C. HORSLEY, A.R.A., G. HICKS, R. REDGRAVE, R.A., C. STONEHOUSE, F. TAYLER, G. THOMAS, H. J. TOWNSHEND, E. H. WEHNERT, HARRISON WEIR, &c.

Bloomfield's Farmer's Boy.	Milton's L'Allegro.
Campbell's Pleasures of Hope.	Poetry of Nature. Harrison Weir.
Coleridge's Ancient Mariner.	Rogers' (Sam.) Pleasures of Memory.
Goldsmith's Deserted Village.	Shakespeare's Songs and Sonnets.
Goldsmith's Vicar of Wakefield.	Tennyson's May Queen.
Gray's Elegy in a Churchyard.	Elizabethan Poets.
Keat's Eve of St. Agnes.	Wordsworth's Pastoral Poems.

" Such works are a glorious beatification for a poet."—*Athenæum.*

Christ in Song. By Dr. PHILIP SCHAFF. A New Edition, Revised, cloth, gilt edges, 6s.

Cobbett (William). A Biography. By EDWARD SMITH. 2 vols., crown 8vo, 25s.

Comedy (The) of Europe, 1860—1890. A retrospective and prospective Sketch. Crown 8vo, 6s.

Conflict of Christianity with Heathenism. By Dr. GERHARD UHLHORN. Edited and Translated from the Third German Edition by G. C. SMYTH and C. J. H. ROPES. 8vo, cloth extra, 10s. 6d.

Continental Tour of Eight Days for Forty-four Shillings. By a JOURNEY-MAN. 12mo, 1s.
> "The book is simply delightful."—*Spectator.*

Corea (The). See "Forbidden Land."

Covert Side Sketches: Thoughts on Hunting, with Different Packs in Different Countries. By J. NEVITT FITT (H.H. of the *Sporting Gazette*, late of the *Field*). 2nd Edition. Crown 8vo, cloth, 10s. 6d.

Crade-Land of Arts and Creeds; or, Nothing New under the Sun. By CHARLES J. STONE, Barrister-at-law, and late Advocate, High Courts, Bombay, 8vo, pp. 420, cloth, 14s.

Cripps the Carrier. 3rd Edition, 6s. See BLACKMORE.

Cruise of H.M.S. "Challenger" (The). By W. J. J. SPRY, R.N. With Route Map and many Illustrations. 6th Edition, demy 8vo, cloth, 18s. Cheap Edition, crown 8vo, some of the Illustrations, 7s. 6d.

Curious Adventures of a Field Cricket. By Dr. ERNEST CANDÈZE. Translated by N. D'ANVERS. With numerous fine Illustrations. Crown 8vo, cloth extra, gilt edges, 7s. 6d.

DANA (R. H.) Two Years before the Mast and Twenty-Four years After. Revised Edition with Notes, 12mo, 6s.

Daughter (A) of Heth. By W. BLACK. Crown 8vo, 6s.

Day of My Life (A); or, Every Day Experiences at Eton. By an ETON BOY, Author of "About Some Fellows." 16mo, cloth extra, 2s. 6d. 6th Thousand.

Day out of the Life of a Little Maiden (A): Six Studies from Life. By SHERER and ENGLER. Large 4to, in portfolio, 5s.

Diane. By Mrs. MACQUOID. Crown 8vo, 6s.

Dick Cheveley: his Fortunes and Misfortunes. By W. H. G. KINGSTON. 350 pp., square 16mo, and 22 full-page Illustrations. Cloth, gilt edges, 7s. 6d.

Dick Sands, the Boy Captain. By JULES VERNE. With nearly 100 Illustrations, cloth extra, gilt edges, 10s. 6d.

Dodge (*Mrs. M.*) *Hans Brinker; or, the Silver Skates.* An entirely New Edition, with 59 Full-page and other Woodcuts. Square crown 8vo, cloth extra, 5*s.* ; Text only, paper, 1*s.*

Dogs of Assize. A Legal Sketch-Book in Black and White. Containing 6 Drawings by WALTER J. ALLEN. Folio, in wrapper, 6*s.* 8*d.*

*E*IGHT *Cousins.* See ALCOTT.

Eldmuir: An Art-Story of Scottish Home-Life, Scenery, and Incident. By JACOB THOMPSON, Jun. Illustrated with Engravings after Paintings of JACOB THOMPSON. With an Introductory Notice by LLEWELLYNN JEWITT, F.S.A., &c. Demy 8vo, cloth extra, 14*s.*

Elinor Dryden. By Mrs. MACQUOID. Crown 8vo, 6*s.*

Embroidery (*Handbook of*). By L. HIGGIN. Edited by LADY MARIAN ALFORD, and published by authority of the Royal School of Art Needlework. With 16 page Illustrations, Designs for Borders, &c. Crown 8vo, 5*s.*

English Catalogue of Books (*The*). Published during 1863 to 1871 inclusive, comprising also important American Publications. 30*s.*

*** Of the previous Volume, 1835 to 1862, very few remain on sale ; as also of the Index Volume, 1837 to 1857.

—— *Supplements*, 1863, 1864, 1865, 3*s.* 6*d.* each; 1866 to 1880, 5*s.* each.

English Writers, Chapters for Self-Improvement in English Literature. By the Author of "The Gentle Life," 6*s.* ; smaller edition, 2*s.* 6*d.*

English Philosophers. A Series of Volumes containing short biographies of the most celebrated English Philosophers, designed to direct the reader to the sources of more detailed and extensive criticism than the size and nature of the books in this Series would permit. Though not issued in chronological order, the series will, when complete, constitute a comprehensive history of English Philosophy. Two Volumes will be issued simultaneously at brief intervals, in square 16mo, price 2*s.* 6*d.*

The following are already arranged :—

Bacon. Professor FOWLER, Professor of Logic in Oxford.

Berkeley. Professor T. H. GREEN, Professor of Moral Philosophy, Oxford.

Hamilton. Professor MONK, Professor of Moral Philosophy, Dublin.

J. S. Mill. Miss HELEN TAYLOR, Editor of "The Works of Buckle," &c.

Mansel. Rev. J. H. HUCKIN, D.D., Head Master of Repton.

Adam Smith. Mr. J. A. FARRER, M.A., Author of "Primitive Manners and Customs."

English Philosophers, continued :—

Hobbes. Mr. A. H. GOSSET, B.A., Fellow of New College, Oxford.
Bentham. Mr. G. E. BUCKLE, M.A., Fellow of All Souls', Oxford.
Austin. Mr. HARRY JOHNSON, B.A., late Scholar of Queen's College, Oxford.
Hartley. } Mr. E. S. BOWEN, B.A., late Scholar of New College,
James Mill. } Oxford.
Shaftesbury. } Professor FOWLER.
Hutcheson. }

Erchomenon ; or, The Republic of Materialism. Small post 8vo, cloth, 5s.

Erema ; or, My Father's Sin. *See* BLACKMORE.

Eton. *See* " Day of my Life," " Out of School," " About Some Fellows."

Evans (C.) Over the Hills and Far Away. By C. EVANS. One Volume, crown 8vo, cloth extra, 10s. 6d.

——— *A Strange Friendship.* Crown 8vo, cloth, 5s.

*F*AMILY *Prayers for Working Men.* By the Author of " Steps to the Throne of Grace." With an Introduction by the Rev. E. H. BICKERSTETH, M.A. Cloth, 1s. ; sewed, 6d.

Fern Paradise (The): A Plea for the Culture of Ferns. By F. G. HEATH. New Edition, entirely Rewritten, Illustrated with Eighteen full-page, numerous other Woodcuts, including 8 Plates of Ferns and Four Photographs, large post 8vo, cloth, gilt edges, 12s. 6d. Sixth Edition. In 12 Parts, sewn, 1s. each.

  " This charming Volume will not only enchant the Fern-lover, but will also please and instruct the general reader."—*Spectator.*

Fern World (The). By F. G. HEATH. Illustrated by Twelve Coloured Plates, giving complete Figures (Sixty-four in all) of every Species of British Fern, printed from Nature ; by several full-page Engravings. Cloth, gilt, 6th Edition, 12s. 6d. In 12 parts, 1s. each.

  " Mr. HEATH has really given us good, well-written descriptions of our native Ferns, with indications of their habitats, the conditions under which they grow naturally, and under which they may be cultivated."—*Athenæum.*

Few (A) Hints on Proving Wills. Enlarged Edition, 1s.

First Steps in Conversational French Grammar. By F. JULIEN. Being an Introduction to " Petites Leçons de Conversation et de Grammaire," by the same Author. Fcap. 8vo, 128 pp., 1s.

Five Years in Minnesota. By MAURICE FARRAR, M.A. Crown 8vo, cloth extra, 6s.

Flooding of the Sahara (The). *See* MACKENZIE.

Food for the People ; or, Lentils and other Vegetable Cookery. By E. E. ORLEBAR. Third Thousand. Small post 8vo, boards, 1s.

A Fool's Errand. By ONE OF THE FOOLS. Crown 8vo, cloth extra, 5*s*.

Footsteps of the Master. See STOWE (Mrs. BEECHER).

Forbidden Land (A): Voyages to the Corea. By G. OPPERT. Numerous Illustrations and Maps. Demy 8vo, cloth extra, 21*s*.

Four Lectures on Electric Induction. Delivered at the Royal Institution, 1878-9. By J. E. H. GORDON, B.A. Cantab. With numerous Illustrations. Cloth limp, square 16mo, 3*s*.

Foreign Countries and the British Colonies. Edited by F. S. PULLING, M.A., Lecturer at Queen's College, Oxford, and formerly Professor at the Yorkshire College, Leeds. A Series of small Volumes descriptive of the principal Countries of the World by well-known Authors, each Country being treated of by a Writer who from Personal Knowledge is qualified to speak with authority on the Subject. The Volumes will average 180 crown 8vo pages, will contain Maps, and, in some cases, a few typical Illustrations.

The following Volumes are in preparation :—

Denmark and Iceland.	Russia.	Canada.
Greece.	Persia.	Sweden and Norway.
Switzerland.	Japan.	The West Indies.
Austria.	Peru.	New Zealand.

Franc (Maude Jeane). The following form one Series, small post 8vo, in uniform cloth bindings :—

—— *Emily's Choice.* 5*s*.

—— *Hall's Vineyard.* 4*s*.

—— *John's Wife : a Story of Life in South Australia.* 4*s*.

—— *Marian ; or, the Light of Some One's Home.* 5*s*.

—— *Silken Cords and Iron Fetters.* 4*s*.

—— *Vermont Vale.* 5*s*.

—— *Minnie's Mission.* 4*s*.

—— *Little Mercy.* 5*s*.

—— *Beatrice Melton.* 4*s*.

Friends and Foes in the Transkei : An Englishwoman's Experiences during the Cape Frontier War of 1877-8. By HELEN M. PRICHARD. Crown 8vo, cloth, 10*s*. 6*d*.

Froissart (The Boy's). Selected from the Chronicles of England, France, Spain, &c. By SIDNEY LANIER. The Volume will be fully Illustrated. Crown 8vo, cloth, 7*s*. 6*d*.

Funny Foreigners and Eccentric Englishmen. 16 coloured comic Illustrations for Children. Fcap. folio, coloured wrapper, 4*s*.

GAMES of Patience.   See CADOGAN.

Gentle Life (Queen Edition).   2 vols. in 1, small 4to, 10s. 6d.

THE GENTLE LIFE SERIES.

Price 6s. each ; or in calf extra, price 10s. 6d. ; Smaller Edition, cloth
extra, 2s. 6d.

A Reprint (with the exception of "Familiar Words" and "Other
People's Windows") has been issued in very neat limp cloth bindings
at 2s. 6d. each.

The Gentle Life.   Essays in aid of the Formation of Character
of Gentlemen and Gentlewomen.   21st Edition.
"Deserves to be printed in letters of gold, and circulated in every house."—
Chambers' Journal.

About in the World.   Essays by Author of "The Gentle Life."
"It is not easy to open it at any page without finding some handy idea."—*Morning Post.*

Like unto Christ.   A New Translation of Thomas à Kempis'
"De Imitatione Christi."   2nd Edition.
"Could not be presented in a more exquisite form, for a more sightly volume was
never seen."—*Illustrated London News.*

Familiar Words.   An Index Verborum, or Quotation Handbook.   Affording an immediate Reference to Phrases and Sentences
that have become embedded in the English language.   3rd and
enlarged Edition.   6s.
"The most extensive dictionary of quotation we have met with."—*Notes and
Queries.*

Essays by Montaigne.   Edited and Annotated by the Author
of "The Gentle Life."   With Portrait.   2nd Edition.
"We should be glad if any words of ours could help to bespeak a large circula-
tion for this handsome attractive book."—*Illustrated Times.*

The Countess of Pembroke's Arcadia.   Written by Sir PHILIP
SIDNEY.   Edited with Notes by Author of "The Gentle Life."   7s. 6d.
"All the best things are retained intact in Mr. Friswell's edition."—*Examiner.*

The Gentle Life.   2nd Series, 8th Edition.
"There is not a single thought in the volume that does not contribute in some
measure to the formation of a true gentleman."—*Daily News.*

The Silent Hour: Essays, Original and Selected.   By the
Author of "The Gentle Life."   3rd Edition.
"All who possess 'The Gentle Life' should own this volume."—*Standard.*

Half-Length Portraits.   Short Studies of Notable Persons.
By J. HAIN FRISWELL.   Small post 8vo, cloth extra, 6s.

Essays on English Writers, for the Self-improvement of
Students in English Literature.
"To all who have neglected to read and study their native literature we would
certainly suggest the volume before us as a fitting introduction."—*Examiner.*

The Gentle Life Series (continued):—

Other People's Windows. By J. HAIN FRISWELL. 3rd Edition.
"The chapters are so lively in themselves, so mingled with shrewd views of human nature, so full of illustrative anecdotes, that the reader cannot fail to be amused."—*Morning Post.*

A Man's Thoughts. By J. HAIN FRISWELL.

German Primer. Being an Introduction to First Steps in German. By M. T. PREU. 2s. 6d.

Getting On in the World; or, Hints on Success in Life. By W. MATHEWS, LL.D. Small post 8vo, cloth, 2s. 6d.; gilt edges, 3s. 6d.

Gilpin's Forest Scenery. Edited by F. G. HEATH. Large post 8vo, with numerous Illustrations. Uniform with "The Fern World" and "Our Woodland Trees." 12s. 6d.
"Those who know Mr. HEATH's Volumes on Ferns, as well as his 'Woodland Trees,' and his little work on 'Burnham Beeches,' will understand the enthusiasm with which he has executed his task. . . . The Volume deserves to be a favourite in the boudoir as well as in the library."—*Saturday Review.*

Gordon (J. E. H.). See "Four Lectures on Electric Induction," "Physical Treatise on Electricity," &c.

Gouffé. The Royal Cookery Book. By JULES GOUFFÉ; translated and adapted for English use by ALPHONSE GOUFFÉ, Head Pastrycook to her Majesty the Queen. Illustrated with large plates printed in colours. 161 Woodcuts, 8vo, cloth extra, gilt edges, 2l. 2s.

—— Domestic Edition, half-bound, 10s. 6d.
"By far the ablest and most complete work on cookery that has eve been submitted to the gastronomical world."—*Pall Mall Gazette.*

Gouraud (Mdlle.) Four Gold Pieces. Numerous Illustrations. Small post 8vo, cloth, 2s. 6d. See also Rose Library.

Government of M. Thiers. By JULES SIMON. Translated from the French. 2 vols., demy 8vo, cloth extra, 32s.

Great Artists. See Biographies.

Greek Grammar. See WALLER.

Guizot's History of France. Translated by ROBERT BLACK. Super-royal 8vo, very numerous Full-page and other Illustrations. In 5 vols., cloth extra, gilt, each 24s.
"It supplies a want which has long been felt, and ought to be in the hands of all students of history."—*Times.*

—— *Masson's School Edition.* The History of France from the Earliest Times to the Outbreak of the Revolution; abridged from the Translation by Robert Black, M.A., with Chronological Index, Historical and Genealogical Tables, &c. By Professor GUSTAVE MASSON, B.A., Assistant Master at Harrow School. With 24 full-page Portraits, and many other Illustrations. 1 vol., demy 8vo, 600 pp., cloth extra, 10s. 6d.

Guizot's History of England. In 3 vols. of about 500 pp. each, containing 60 to 70 Full-page and other Illustrations, cloth extra, gilt, 24*s.* each.

"For luxury of typography, plainness of print, and beauty of illustration, these volumes, of which but one has as yet appeared in English, will hold their own against any production of an age so luxurious as our own in everything, typography not excepted."—*Times.*

Guyon (Mde.) Life. By UPHAM. 6th Edition, crown 8vo, 6*s.*

HANDBOOK to the Charities of London. See Low's.

—— *of Embroidery ; which see.*

—— *to the Principal Schools of England.* See Practical.

Half-Hours of Blind Man's Holiday ; or, Summer and Winter Sketches in Black & White. By W. W. FENN. 2 vols., cr. 8vo, 24*s.*

Half-Length Portraits. Short Studies of Notable Persons. By J. HAIN FRISWELL. Small post 8vo, 6*s.* ; Smaller Edition, 2*s.* 6*d.*

Hall (W. W.) How to Live Long ; or, 1408 *Health Maxims,* Physical, Mental, and Moral. By W. W. HALL, A.M., M.D. Small post 8vo, cloth, 2*s.* Second Edition.

Hans Brinker ; or, the Silver Skates. See DODGE.

Have I a Vote ? A Handy Book for the Use of the People, on the Qualifications conferring the Right of Voting at County and Borough Parliamentary Elections. With Forms and Notes. By T. H. LEWIS, B.A., LL.B. Paper, 6*d.*

Heart of Africa. Three Years' Travels and Adventures in the Unexplored Regions of Central Africa, from 1868 to 1871. By Dr. GEORG SCHWEINFURTH. Numerous Illustrations, and large Map. 2 vols., crown 8vo, cloth, 15*s.*

Heath (Francis George). See "Fern World," "Fern Paradise," "Our Woodland Trees," "Trees and Ferns;" "Gilpin's Forest Scenery," "Burnham Beeches," "Sylvan Spring," &c.

Heber's (Bishop) Illustrated Edition of Hymns. With upwards of 100 beautiful Engravings. Small 4to, handsomely bound, 7*s.* 6*d.* Morocco, 18*s.* 6*d.* and 21*s.* An entirely New Edition.

Hector Servadac. See VERNE. 10*s.* 6*d.* and 5*s.*

Heir of Kilfinnan (The). New Story by W. H. G. KINGSTON, Author of "Snoe Shoes and Canoes," "With Axe and Rifle," &c. With Illustrations. Cloth, gilt edges, 7*s.* 6*d.*

History and Handbook of Photography. Translated from the French of GASTON TISSANDIER. Edited by J. THOMSON. Imperial 16mo, over 300 pages, 70 Woodcuts, and Specimens of Prints by the best Permanent Processes. Second Edition, with an Appendix by the late Mr. HENRY FOX TALBOT. Cloth extra, 6*s.*

History of a Crime (The) ; Deposition of an Eye-witness. By VICTOR HUGO. 4 vols., crown 8vo, 42s. Cheap Edition, 1 vol., 6s.

———— *England.* See GUIZOT.

———— *France.* See GUIZOT.

———— *of Russia.* ee RAMBAUD.

———— *Merchant Shipping.* See LINDSAY.

———— *United States.* See BRYANT.

———— *Ireland.* STANDISH O'GRADY. Vols. I. and II., 7s. 6d. each.

———— *American Literature.* By M. C. TYLER. Vols. I. and II., 2 vols, 8vo, 24s.

History and Principles of Weaving by Hand and by Power. With several hundred Illustrations. By ALFRED BARLOW. Royal 8vo, cloth extra, 1l. 5s. Second Edition.

Hitherto. By the Author of " The Gayworthys." New Edition, cloth extra, 3s. 6d. Also, in Rose Library, 2 vols., 2s.

Home of the Eddas. By C. G. LOCK. Demy 8vo, cloth, 16s.

How to Live Long. See HALL.

How to get Strong and how to Stay so. By WILLIAM BLAIKIE. A Manual of Rational, Physical, Gymnastic, and other Exercises. With Illustrations, small post 8vo, 5s.

"Worthy of every one's attention, whether old or young."—*Graphic.*

Hugo (Victor) "*Ninety-Three.*" Illustrated. Crown 8vo, 6s.

———— *Toilers of the Sea.* Crown 8vo. Illustrated, 6s.; fancy boards, 2s.; cloth, 2s. 6d.; On large paper with all the original Illustrations, 10s. 6d.

————. *See* "History of a Crime."

Hundred Greatest Men (The). 8 vols., containing 15 to 20 Portraits each, 21s. each. See below.

"Messrs. SAMPSON LOW & Co. are about to issue an important 'International' work, entitled, 'THE HUNDRED GREATEST MEN;' being the Lives and Portraits of the 100 Greatest Men of History, divided into Eight Classes, each Class to form a Monthly Quarto Volume. The Introductions to the volumes are to be written by recognized authorities on the different subjects, the English contributors being DEAN STANLEY, Mr. MATTHEW ARNOLD, Mr. FROUDE, and Professor MAX MÜLLER: in Germany, Professor HELMHOLTZ; in France, MM. TAINE and RENAN; and in America, Mr. EMERSON. The Portraits are to be Reproductions from fine and rare Steel Engravings."—*Academy.*

Hygiene and Public Health (A Treatise on). Edited by A. H. BUCK, M.D. Illustrated by numerous Wood Engravings. In 2 royal 8vo vols., cloth, one guinea each.

Hymnal Companion to Book of Common Prayer. See BICKERSTETH.

ILLUSTRATED Text-Books of Art-Education. A Series of Monthly Volumes preparing for publication. Edited by EDWARD J. POYNTER, R.A., Director for Art, Science and Art Department.

The first Volumes, large crown 8vo, cloth, 3s. 6d. each, will be issued in the following divisions:—

PAINTING.

Classic and Italian. | French and Spanish.
German, Flemish, and Dutch. | English and American.

ARCHITECTURE.

Classic and Early Christian. | Gothic, Renaissance, & Modern.

SCULPTURE.

Classic and Oriental. | Renaissance and Modern.

ORNAMENT.

Decoration in Colour. | Architectural Ornament.

Illustrations of China and its People. By J. THOMPSON F.R.G.S. Four Volumes, imperial 4to, each 3l. 3s.

In my Indian Garden. By PHIL ROBINSON. With a Preface by EDWIN ARNOLD, M.A., C.S.I., &c. Crown 8vo, limp cloth, 3s. 6d.

Involuntary Voyage (An). Showing how a Frenchman who abhorred the Sea was most unwillingly and by a series of accidents driven round the World. Numerous Illustrations. Square crown 8vo, cloth extra, 7s. 6d.

Irish Bar. Comprising Anecdotes, Bon-Mots, and Biographical Sketches of the Bench and Bar of Ireland. By J. RODERICK O'FLANAGAN, Barrister-at-Law. Crown 8vo, 12s. Second Edition.

JACK and Jill. By Miss ALCOTT. Small post 8vo, cloth, gilt edges, 5s.

Jacquemart (A.) History of the Ceramic Art. By ALBERT JACQUEMART. With 200 Woodcuts, 12 Steel-plate Engravings, and 1000 Marks and Monograms. Translated by Mrs. BURY PALLISER. Super-royal 8vo, cloth extra, gilt edges, 28s.

Jimmy's Cruise in the Pinafore. See ALCOTT.

KAFIRLAND: A Ten Months' Campaign. By FRANK N. STREATFIELD, Resident Magistrate in Kaffraria, and Commandant of Native Levies during the Kaffir War of 1878. Crown 8vo, cloth extra, 7s. 6d.

Keble Autograph Birthday Book (The). Containing on each left-hand page the date and a selected verse from Keble's hymns. Imperial 8vo, with 12 Floral Chromos, ornamental binding, gilt edges, 15s.

Khedive's Egypt (*The*); *or, The old House of Bondage under* New Masters. By EDWIN DE LEON. Illustrated. Demy 8vo, 8*s*. 6*d*.

King's Rifle (*The*): *From the Atlantic to the Indian Ocean;* Across Unknown Countries; Discovery of the Great Zambesi Affluents, &c. By Major SERPA PINTO. With 24 full-page and about 100 smaller Illustrations, 13 small Maps, and 1 large one. Demy 8vo.

Kingston (*W. H. G.*). *See* "Snow-Shoes."

---— *Child of the Cavern.*

---— *Two Supercargoes.*

---— *With Axe and Rifle.*

---— *Begum's Fortune.*

---— *Heir of Kilfinnan.*

---— *Dick Cheveley.*

*L*ADY *Silverdale's Sweetheart.* 6*s*. *See* BLACK.

Lenten Meditations. In Two Series, each complete in itself. By the Rev. CLAUDE BOSANQUET, Author of "Blossoms from the King's Garden." 16mo, cloth, First Series, 1*s*. 6*d*.; Second Series, 2*s*.

Lentils. See "Food for the People."

Liesegang (*Dr. Paul E.*) *A Manual of the Carbon Process of* Photography. Demy 8vo, half-bound, with Illustrations, 4*s*.

Life and Letters of the Honourable Charles Sumner (*The*). 2 vols., royal 8vo, cloth. Second Edition, 36*s*.

Lindsay (*W. S.*) *History of Merchant Shipping and Ancient* Commerce. Over 150 Illustrations, Maps and Charts. In 4 vols., demy 8vo, cloth extra. Vols. 1 and 2, 21*s*.; vols. 3 and 4, 24*s*. each.

Lion Jack: a Story of Perilous Adventures amongst Wild Men and Beasts. Showing how Menageries are made. By P. T. BARNUM. With Illustrations. Crown 8vo, cloth extra, price 6*s*.

Little King; or, the Taming of a Young Russian Count. By S. BLANDY. 64 Illustrations. Crown 8vo, gilt edges, 7*s*. 6*d*.; plainer binding, 5*s*.

Little Mercy; or, For Better for Worse. By MAUDE JEANNE FRANC, Author of "Marian," "Vermont Vale," &c., &c. Small post 8vo, cloth extra, 4*s*. Second Edition.

Long (*Col. C. Chaillé*) *Central Africa.* Naked Truths of Naked People: an Account of Expeditions to Lake Victoria Nyanza and the Mabraka Niam-Niam. Demy 8vo, numerous Illustrations, 18*s*.

Lost Sir Massingberd. New Edition, crown 8vo, boards, coloured wrapper, 2*s*.

Low's German Series—

1. **The Illustrated German Primer.** Being the easiest introduction to the study of German for all beginners.   1*s.*
2. **The Children's own German Book.** A Selection of Amusing and Instructive Stories in Prose. Edited by Dr. A. L. MEISSNER. Small post 8vo, cloth, 1*s.* 6*d.*
3. **The First German Reader, for Children from Ten to Fourteen.** Edited by Dr. A. L. MEISSNER. Small post 8vo, cloth, 1*s.* 6*d.*
4. **The Second German Reader.** Edited by Dr. A. L. MEISSNER. Small post 8vo, cloth, 1*s.* 6*d.*

   Buchheim's Deutsche Prosa.   Two Volumes, sold separately :—

5. **Schiller's Prosa.** Containing Selections from the Prose Works of Schiller, with Notes for English Students. By Dr. BUCHHEIM, Small post 8vo, 2*s.* 6*d.*
6. **Goethe's Prosa.** Selections from the Prose Works of Goethe, with Notes for English Students. By Dr. BUCHHEIM. Small post 8vo, 3*s.* 6*d.*

Low's International Series of Toy Books.   6*d.* each; or Mounted on Linen, 1*s.*

1. **Little Fred and his Fiddle,** from Asbjörnsen's "Norwegian Fairy Tales."
2. **The Lad and the North Wind,**   ditto.
3. **The Pancake,**   ditto.

Low's Standard Library of Travel and Adventure.   Crown 8vo, bound uniformly in cloth extra, price 7*s.* 6*d.*

1. **The Great Lone Land.** By Major W. F. BUTLER, C.B.
2. **The Wild North Land.** By Major W. F. BUTLER, C.B.
3. **How I found Livingstone.** By H. M. STANLEY.
4. **The Threshold of the Unknown Region.** By C. R. MARK-HAM. (4th Edition, with Additional Chapters, 10*s.* 6*d.*)
5. **A Whaling Cruise to Baffin's Bay and the Gulf of Boothia.** By A. H. MARKHAM.
6. **Campaigning on the Oxus.** By J. A. MACGAHAN.
7. **Akim-foo: the History of a Failure.** By MAJOR W. F. BUTLER, C.B.
8. **Ocean to Ocean.** By the Rev. GEORGE M. GRANT. With Illustrations.
9. **Cruise of the Challenger.** By W. J. J. SPRY, R.N.
10. **Schweinfurth's Heart of Africa.** 2 vols., 15*s.*
11. **Through the Dark Continent.** By H. M. STANLEY. 1 vol., 12*s.* 6*d.*

Low's Standard Novels. Crown 8vo, 6s. each, cloth extra.

My Lady Greensleeves. By HELEN MATHERS, Authoress of " Comin' through the Rye," "Cherry Ripe," &c.

Three Feathers. By WILLIAM BLACK.

A Daughter of Heth. 13th Edition. By W. BLACK. With Frontispiece by F. WALKER, A.R.A.

Kilmeny. A Novel. By W. BLACK.

In Silk Attire. By W. BLACK.

Lady Silverdale's Sweetheart. By W. BLACK.

History of a Crime : The Story of the Coup d'État. By VICTOR HUGO.

Alice Lorraine. By R. D. BLACKMORE.

Lorna Doone. By R. D. BLACKMORE. 8th Edition.

Cradock Nowell. By R. D. BLACKMORE.

Clara Vaughan. By R. D. BLACKMORE.

Cripps the Carrier. By R. D. BLACKMORE.

Erema ; or My Father's Sin. By R. D. BLACKMORE.

Innocent. By Mrs. OLIPHANT. Eight Illustrations.

Work. A Story of Experience. By LOUISA M. ALCOTT. Illustra‐ tions. *See also* Rose Library.

The Afghan Knife. By R. A. STERNDALE, Author of " Seonee."

A French Heiress in her own Chateau. By the author of " One Only," "Constantia," &c. Six Illustrations.

Ninety-Three. By VICTOR HUGO. Numerous Illustrations.

My Wife and I. By Mrs. BEECHER STOWE.

Wreck of the Grosvenor. By W. CLARK RUSSELL.

Elinor Dryden. By Mrs. MACQUOID.

Diane. By Mrs. MACQUOID.

Poganuc People, Their Loves and Lives. By Mrs. BEECHER STOWE.

A Golden Sorrow. By Mrs. CASHEL HOEY.

Low's Handbook to the Charities of London. Edited and revised to date by C. MACKESON, F.S.S., Editor of " A Guide to the Churches of London and its Suburbs," &c. 1s.

MACGAHAN (J. A.) Campaigning on the Oxus, and the Fall of Khiva. With Map and numerous Illustrations, 4th Edition, small post 8vo, cloth extra, 7s. 6d.

Macgregor (John) "Rob Roy" on the Baltic. 3rd Edition, small post 8vo, 2s. 6d.

—— *A Thousand Miles in the "Rob Roy" Canoe.* 11th Edition, small post 8vo, 2s. 6d.

Macgregor (John) Description of the "Rob Roy" Canoe, with Plans, &c., 1*s*.

—— *The Voyage Alone in the Yawl "Rob Roy."* New Edition, thoroughly revised, with additions, small post 8vo, 5*s*.; boards, 2*s*. 6*d*.

Mackenzie (D). The Flooding of the Sahara. By DONALD MACKENZIE. 8vo, cloth extra, with Illustrations, 10*s*. 6*d*.

Macquoid (Mrs.) Elinor Dryden. Crown 8vo, cloth, 6*s*.

—— *Diane.* Crown 8vo, 6*s*.

Magazine (Illustrated) for Young People. See "St. Nicholas."

Markham (C. R.) The Threshold of the Unknown Region. Crown 8vo, with Four Maps, 4th Edition. Cloth extra, 10*s*. 6*d*.

Maury (Commander) Physical Geography of the Sea, and its Meteorology. Being a Reconstruction and Enlargement of his former Work, with Charts and Diagrams. New Edition, crown 8vo, 6*s*.

Memoirs of Madame de Rémusat, 1802—1808. By her Grandson, M. PAUL DE RÉMUSAT, Senator. Translated by Mrs. CASHEL HOEY and and Mr. JOHN LILLIE. 4th Edition, cloth extra. This work was written by Madame de Rémusat during the time she was living on the most intimate terms with the Empress Josephine, and is full of revelations respecting the private life of Bonaparte, and of men and politics of the first years of the century. Revelations which have already created a great sensation in Paris. 8vo, 2 vols. 32*s*.

Men of Mark : a Gallery of Contemporary Portraits of the most Eminent Men of the Day taken from Life, especially for this publication, price 1*s*. 6*d*. monthly. Vols. I., II., III., and IV., handsomely bound, cloth, gilt edges, 25*s*. each.

Michael Strogoff. 10*s*. 6*d*. and 5*s*. *See* VERNE.

Mitford (Miss). See "Our Village."

Montaigne's Essays. See "Gentle Life Series."

My Brother Jack ; or, The Story of Whatd'yecallem. Written by Himself. From the French of ALPHONSE DAUDET. Illustrated by P. PHILIPPOTEAUX. Imperial 16mo, cloth extra, gilt edges, 7*s*. 6*d*.; plainer binding, 5*s*.

My Lady Greensleeves. By HELEN MATHERS, Authoress of "'Comin' through the Rye," "Cherry Ripe," &c. 1 vol. edition, crown 8vo, cloth, 6*s*.

My Rambles in the New World. By LUCIEN BIART, Author of "The Adventures of a Young Naturalist." Numerous full-page Illustrations. Crown 8vo, cloth extra, gilt edges, 7s. 6d. ; plainer binding, 5s.

Mysterious Island. By JULES VERNE. 3 vols., imperial 16mo. 150 Illustrations, cloth gilt, 3s. 6d. each ; elaborately bound, gilt edges, 7s. 6d. each. Cheap Edition, with some of the Illustrations, cloth, gilt, 2s. ; paper, 1s. each.

NARES (Sir G. S., K.C.B.) Narrative of a Voyage to the Polar Sea during 1875-76, in H.M.'s Ships "Alert" and "Discovery." By Captain Sir G. S. NARES, R.N., K.C.B., F.R.S. Published by permission of the Lords Commissioners of the Admiralty. With Notes on the Natural History, edited by H. W. FEILDEN, F.G.S., C.M.Z.S., F.R.G.S., Naturalist to the Expedition. Two Volumes, demy 8vo, with numerous Woodcut Illustrations, Photographs, &c. 4th Edition, 2l. 2s.

National Music of the World. By the late HENRY F. CHORLEY. Edited by H. G. HEWLETT. Crown 8vo, cloth, 8s. 6d.

"What I have to offer are not a few impressions, scrambled together in the haste of the moment, but are the result of many years of comparison and experience."— *From the Author's "Prelude."*

New Child's Play (A). Sixteen Drawings by E. V. B. Beautifully printed in colours, 4to, cloth extra, 12s. 6d.

New Guinea (A Few Months in). By OCTAVIUS C. STONE, F.R.G.S. With numerous Illustrations from the Author's own Drawings. Crown 8vo, cloth, 12s.

New Ireland. By A. M. SULLIVAN, M.P. for Louth. 2 vols., demy 8vo, 30s. Cheaper Edition, 1 vol., crown 8vo, 8s. 6d.

New Novels. Crown 8vo, cloth, 10s. 6d. per vol. :—

Mary Anerley. By R. D. BLACKMORE, Author of "Lorna Doone," &c. 3 vols.

The Sisters. By G. EBERS, Author of "An Egyptian Princess." 2 vols., 16mo, 2s. each.

Countess Daphne. By RITA, Authoress of ",Vivienne" and "Like Dian's Kiss." 3 vols.

Sunrise. By W. BLACK. In 15 Monthly Parts, 1s. each.

Wait a Year. By HARRIET BOWRA, Authoress of "A Young Wife's Story." 3 vols.

Sarah de Beranger. By JEAN INGELOW. 3 vols.

The Braes of Yarrow. By C. GIBBON. 3 vols.

Elaine's Story. By MAUD SHERIDAN. 2 vols.

Prince Fortune and His Friends. 3 vols.

Noble Words and Noble Deeds. Translated from the French of
E. MULLER, by DORA LEIGH. Containing many Full-page Illustrations by PHILIPPOTEAUX. Square imperial 16mo, cloth extra, 7s. 6d.

North American Review (The). Monthly, price 2s. 6d.

Notes on Fish and Fishing. By the Rev. J. J. MANLEY, M.A.
With Illustrations, crown 8vo, cloth extra, leatherette binding, 10s. 6d.

Nursery Playmates (Prince of). 217 Coloured pictures for
Children by eminent Artists. Folio, in coloured boards, 6s.

OBERAMMERGAU Passion Play. See "Art in the
Mountains."

Ocean to Ocean: Sandford Fleming's Expedition through
Canada in 1872. By the Rev. GEORGE M. GRANT. With Illustrations. Revised and enlarged Edition, crown 8vo, cloth, 7s. 6d.

Old-Fashioned Girl. See ALCOTT.

Oliphant (Mrs.) Innocent. A Tale of Modern Life. By Mrs.
OLIPHANT, Author of "The Chronicles of Carlingford," &c., &c.
With Eight Full-page Illustrations, small post 8vo, cloth extra, 6s.

On Horseback through Asia Minor. By Capt. FRED BURNABY,
Royal Horse Guards, Author of "A Ride to Khiva." 2 vols.,
8vo, with three Maps and Portrait of Author, 6th Edition, 38s.;
Cheaper Edition, crown 8vo, 10s. 6d.

Our Little Ones in Heaven. Edited by the Rev. H. ROBBINS.
With Frontispiece after Sir JOSHUA REYNOLDS. Fcap., cloth extra,
New Edition—the 3rd, with Illustrations, 5s.

Our Village. By MARY RUSSELL MITFORD. Illustrated with
Frontispiece Steel Engraving, and 12 full-page and 157 smaller Cuts
of Figure Subjects and Scenes. Crown 4to, cloth, gilt edges, 21s.

Our Woodland Trees. By F. G. HEATH. Large post 8vo,
cloth, gilt edges, uniform with "Fern World" and "Fern Paradise,"
by the same Author. 8 Coloured Plates (showing leaves of every
British Tree) and 20 Woodcuts, cloth, gilt edges, 12s. 6d. Third
Edition.

"The book, as a whole, meets a distinct need ; its engravings are excellent, its
coloured leaves and leaflets singularly accurate, and both author and engraver
appear to have been animated by a kindred love of their subject."—*Saturday
Review.*

PAINTERS of All Schools. By LOUIS VIARDOT, and other Writers. 500 pp., super-royal 8vo, 20 Full-page and 70 smaller Engravings, cloth extra, 25*s.* A New Edition is issued in Half-crown parts, with fifty additional portraits, cloth, gilt edges, 31*s.* 6*d.*

Palliser (*Mrs.*) *A History of Lace, from the Earliest Period.* A New and Revised Edition, with additional cuts and text, upwards of 100 Illustrations and coloured Designs. 1 vol. 8vo, 1*l.* 1*s.*

"One of the most readable books óf the season ; permanently valuable, always interesting, often amusing, and not inferior in all the essentials of a gift book."—*Times.*

——— *Historic Devices, Badges, and War Cries.* 8vo, 1*l.* 1*s.*

——— *The China Collector's Pocket Companion.* With upwards of 1000 Illustrations of Marks and Monograms. 2nd Edition, with Additions. Small post 8vo, limp cloth, 5*s.*

Petites Leçons de Conversation et de Grammaire: Oral and Conversational Method ; being Lessons introducing the most Useful Topics of Conversation, upon an entirely new principle, &c. By F. JULIEN, French Master at King Edward the Sixth's School, Birmingham. Author of "The Student's French Examiner," "First Steps in Conversational French Grammar," which see.

Phillips (*L.*) *Dictionary of Biographical Reference.* 8vo, 1*l.* 11*s.* 6*d.*

Photography (*History and Handbook of*). *See* TISSANDIER.

Physical Treatise on Electricity and Magnetism. By J. E. H. GORDON, B.A. With about 200 coloured, full-page, and other Illustrations. Among the newer portions of the work may be enumerated : All the more recent investigations on Striæ by Spottiswoode, De la Rue, Moulton, &c. An account of Mr. Crooke's recent researches. Full descriptions and pictures of all the modern Magnetic Survey Instruments now used at Kew Observatory. Full accounts of all the modern work on Specific Inductive Capacity, and of the more recent determination of the ratio of Electric units (v). It is believed that in respect to the number and beauty of the Illustrations, the work will be quite unique. 2 vols., 8vo, 36*s.*

Picture Gallery of British Art (*The*). 38 Permanent Photographs after the most celebrated English Painters. With Descriptive Letterpress. Vols. 1 to 5, cloth extra, 18*s.* each. Vols. 6, 7, and 8, commencing New Series, demy folio, 31*s.* 6*d.*

Pinto (*Major Serpa*). *See* "King's Rifle."

Placita Anglo-Normannica. *The Procedure and Constitution of* the Anglo-Norman Courts (WILLIAM I.—RICHARD I.), as shown by Contemporaneous Records. With Explanatory Notes, &c. By M. M. BIGELOW. Demy 8vo, cloth, 21*s.*

Plutarch's Lives. An Entirely New and Library Edition. Edited by A. H. CLOUGH, Esq. 5 vols., 8vo, 2*l.* 10*s.*; half-morocco, gilt top, 3*l.* Also in 1 vol., royal 8vo, 800 pp., cloth extra, 18*s.*; half-bound, 21*s.*

———— *Morals.* Uniform with Clough's Edition of "Lives of Plutarch." Edited by Professor GOODWIN. 5 vols., 8vo, 3*l.* 3*s.*

Poems of the Inner Life. A New Edition, Revised, with many additional Poems. Small post 8vo, cloth, 5*s.*

Poganuc People: their Loves and Lives. By Mrs. BEECHER STOWE. Crown 8vo, cloth, 6*s.*

Polar Expeditions. *See* KOLDEWEY, MARKHAM, MACGAHAN, and NARES.

Practical (A) Handbook to the Principal Schools of England. By C. E. PASCOE. New Edition, crown 8vo, cloth extra, 3*s.* 6*d.*

Prejevalsky (N. M.) From Kulja, across the Tian Shan to Lob-nor. Translated by E. DELMAR MORGAN, F.R.G.S. Demy 8vo, with a Map. 16*s.*

Prince Ritto ; or, The Four-leaved Shamrock. By FANNY W. CURREY. With 10 Full-page Fac-simile Reproductions of Original Drawings by HELEN O'HARA. Demy 4to, cloth extra, gilt, 10*s.* 6*d.*

Publishers' Circular (The), and General Record of British and Foreign Literature. Published on the 1st and 15th of every Month, 3*d.*

RAMBAUD (Alfred). History of Russia, from its Origin to the Year 1877. With Six Maps. Translated by Mrs. L. B. LANG. 2 vols., demy 8vo, cloth extra, 38*s.*

Recollections of Writers. By CHARLES and MARY COWDEN CLARKE. Authors of "The Concordance to Shakespeare," &c. ; with Letters of CHARLES LAMB, LEIGH HUNT, DOUGLAS JERROLD, and CHARLES DICKENS ; and a Preface by MARY COWDEN CLARKE. Crown 8vo, cloth, 10*s.* 6*d.*

Reminiscences of the War in New Zealand. By THOMAS W. GUDGEON, Lieutenant and Quartermaster, Colonial Forces, N.Z. With Twelve Portraits. Crown 8vo, cloth extra, 10*s.* 6*d.*

Rémusat (Madame de). See "Memoirs of."

Robinson (Phil). See "In my Indian Garden."

Rochefoucauld's Reflections. Bayard Series, 2*s.* 6*d.*

Rogers (S.) Pleasures of Memory. *See* "Choice Editions of Choice Books." *2s. 6d.*

Rose in Bloom. *See* ALCOTT.

Rose Library (The). Popular Literature of all countries. Each volume, *1s.* ; cloth, *2s. 6d.* Many of the Volumes are Illustrated—

1. **Sea-Gull Rock.** By JULES SANDEAU. Illustrated.
2. **Little Women.** By LOUISA M. ALCOTT.
3. **Little Women Wedded.** Forming a Sequel to "Little Women."
4. **The House on Wheels.** By MADAME DE STOLZ. Illustrated.
5. **Little Men.** By LOUISA M. ALCOTT. Dble. vol., *2s.* ; cloth, *3s. 6d.*
6. **The Old-Fashioned Girl.** By LOUISA M. ALCOTT. Double vol., *2s.* ; cloth, *3s. 6d.*
7. **The Mistress of the Manse.** By J. G. HOLLAND.
8. **Timothy Titcomb's Letters to Young People, Single and Married.**
9. **Undine, and the Two Captains.** By Baron DE LA MOTTE FOUQUÉ. A New Translation by F. E. BUNNETT. Illustrated.
10. **Draxy Miller's Dowry, and the Elder's Wife.** By SAXE HOLM.
11. **The Four Gold Pieces.** By Madame GOURAUD. Numerous Illustrations.
12. **Work.** A Story of Experience. First Portion. By LOUISA M. ALCOTT.
13. **Beginning Again.** Being a Continuation of "Work." By LOUISA M. ALCOTT.
14. **Picciola; or, the Prison Flower.** By X. B. SAINTINE. Numerous Graphic Illustrations.
15. **Robert's Holidays.** Illustrated.
16. **The Two Children of St. Domingo.** Numerous Illustrations.
17. **Aunt Jo's Scrap Bag.**
18. **Stowe (Mrs. H. B.) The Pearl of Orr's Island.**
19. —— **The Minister's Wooing.**
20. —— **Betty's Bright Idea.**
21. —— **The Ghost in the Mill.**
22. —— **Captain Kidd's Money.**
23. —— **We and our Neighbours.** Double vol., *2s.*
24. —— **My Wife and I.** Double vol., *2s.* ; cloth, gilt, *3s. 6d.*
25. **Hans Brinker; or, the Silver Skates.**
26. **Lowell's My Study Window.**
27. **Holmes (O. W.) The Guardian Angel.**
28. **Warner (C. D.) My Summer in a Garden.**

The Rose Library, continued :—

29. **Hitherto.** By the Author of "The Gayworthys." 2 vols., 1*s*. each.
30. **Helen's Babies.** By their Latest Victim.
31. **The Barton Experiment.** By the Author of "Helen's Babies."
32. **Dred.** By Mrs. BEECHER STOWE. Double vol., 2*s*.   Cloth, gilt, 3*s*. 6*d*.
33. **Warner (C. D.) In the Wilderness.**
34. **Six to One.** A Seaside Story.

Russell (W. H., LL.D.) The Tour of the Prince of Wales in India. By W. H. RUSSELL, LL.D. Fully Illustrated by SYDNEY P. HALL, M.A. Super-royal 8vo, cloth extra, gilt edges, 52*s*. 6*d*.; Large Paper Edition, 84*s*.

SANCTA Christina: a Story of the First Century. By ELEANOR E. ORLEBAR. With a Preface by the Bishop of Winchester. Small post 8vo, cloth extra, 5*s*.

Scientific Memoirs: being Experimental Contributions to a Knowledge of Radiant Energy. By JOHN WILLIAM DRAPER, M.D., LL.D., Author of "A Treatise on Human Physiology," &c. With Steel Portrait of the Author. Demy 8vo, cloth, 473 pages, 14*s*.

Scott (Sir G. Gilbert.)   See "Autobiography."

Sea-Gull Rock. By JULES SANDEAU, of the French Academy. Royal 16mo, with 79 Illustrations, cloth extra, gilt edges, 7*s*. 6*d*. Cheaper Edition, cloth gilt, 2*s*. 6*d*. *See also* Rose Library.

Seonee: Sporting in the Satpura Range of Central India, and in the Valley of the Nerbudda. By R. A. STERNDALE, F.R.G.S. 8vo, with numerous Illustrations, 21*s*.

The Serpent Charmer: a Tale of the Indian Mutiny. By LOUIS ROUSSELET, Author of "India and its Native Princes." Numerous Illustrations. Crown 8vo, cloth extra, gilt edges, 7*s*. 6*d*. ; plainer binding, 5*s*.

Shakespeare (The Boudoir). Edited by HENRY CUNDELL. Carefully bracketted for reading aloud ; freed from all objectionable matter, and altogether free from notes. Price 2*s*. 6*d*. each volume, cloth extra, gilt edges. Contents :—Vol I., Cymbeline—Merchant of Venice. Each play separately, paper cover, 1*s*. Vol. II., As You Like It—King Lear—Much Ado about Nothing. Vol. III., Romeo and Juliet—Twelfth Night—King John. The latter six plays separately, paper cover, 9*d*.

Shakespeare Key (The). Forming a Companion to "The Complete Concordance to Shakespeare." By CHARLES and MARY COWDEN CLARKE. Demy 8vo, 800 pp., 21*s.*

Shooting: its Appliances, Practice, and Purpose. By JAMES DALZIEL DOUGALL, F.S.A., F.Z.A. Author of "Scottish Field Sports," &c. Crown 8vo, cloth extra, 10*s.* 6*d.*
"The book is admirable in every way. . . . . We wish it every success."—*Globe.*
"A very complete treatise. . . . . Likely to take high rank as an authority on shooting."—*Daily News.*

Silent Hour (The). See "Gentle Life Series."

Silver Pitchers. See ALCOTT.

Simon (Jules). See "Government of M. Thiers."

Six to One. A Seaside Story. 16mo, boards, 1*s.*

Smith (G.) Assyrian Explorations and Discoveries. By the late GEORGE SMITH. Illustrated by Photographs and Woodcuts. Demy 8vo, 6th Edition, 18*s.*

—— *The Chaldean Account of Genesis.* By the late G. SMITH, of the Department of Oriental Antiquities, British Museum. With many Illustrations. Demy 8vo, cloth extra, 6th Edition, 16*s.*

Snow-Shoes and Canoes ; or, the Adventures of a Fur-Hunter in the Hudson's Bay Territory. By W. H. G. KINGSTON. 2nd Edition. With numerous Illustrations. Square crown 8vo, cloth extra, gilt edges, 7*s.* 6*d.* ; plainer binding, 5*s.*

Songs and Etchings in Shade and Sunshine. By J. E. G. Illustrated with 44 Etchings. Small 4to, cloth, gilt tops, 25*s.*

South Kensington Museum. Monthly 1*s.* See "Art Treasures."

Stanley (H. M.) How I Found Livingstone. Crown 8vo, cloth extra, 7*s.* 6*d.* ; large Paper Edition, 10*s.* 6*d.*

—— *"My Kalulu," Prince, King, and Slave.* A Story from Central Africa. Crown 8vo, about 430 pp., with numerous graphic Illustrations, after Original Designs by the Author. Cloth, 7*s.* 6*d.*

—— *Coomassie and Magdala.* A Story of Two British Campaigns in Africa. Demy 8vo, with Maps and Illustrations, 16*s.*

—— *Through the Dark Continent,* which see.

St. Nicholas Magazine. 4to, in handsome cover. 1*s.* monthly. Annual Volumes, handsomely bound, 15*s.* Its special features are, the great variety and interest of its literary contents, and the beauty and profuseness of its Illustrations, which surpass anything yet attempted in any publication for young people, and the stories are by the best living authors of juvenile literature. Each Part contains, on an average, 50 Illustrations.

Story without an End. From the German of Carové, by the late Mrs. SARAH T. AUSTIN. Crown 4to, with 15 Exquisite Drawings by E. V. B., printed in Colours in Fac-simile of the original Water Colours; and numerous other Illustrations. New Edition, 7s. 6d.

———— square 4to, with Illustrations by HARVEY. 2s. 6d.

Stowe (Mrs. Beecher) Dred. Cheap Edition, boards, 2s. Cloth, gilt edges, 3s. 6d.

———— *Footsteps of the Master.* With Illustrations and red borders. Small post 8vo, cloth extra, 6s.

———— *Geography,* with 60 Illustrations. Square cloth, 4s. 6d.

———— *Little Foxes.* Cheap Edition, 1s.; Library Edition, 4s. 6d.

———— *Betty's Bright Idea.* 1s.

———— *My Wife and I; or, Harry Henderson's History.* Small post 8vo, cloth extra, 6s.*

———— *Minister's Wooing.* 5s.; Copyright Series, 1s. 6d.; cl., 2s.*

———— *Old Town Folk.* 6s.; Cheap Edition, 2s. 6d.

———— *Old Town Fireside Stories.* Cloth extra, 3s. 6d.

———— *Our Folks at Poganuc.* 10s. 6d.

———— *We and our Neighbours.* 1 vol., small post 8vo, 6s. Sequel to "My Wife and I."*

———— *Pink and White Tyranny.* Small post 8vo, 3s. 6d.; Cheap Edition, 1s. 6d. and 2s.

———— *Queer Little People.* 1s.; cloth, 2s.

———— *Chimney Corner.* 1s.; cloth, 1s. 6d.

———— *The Pearl of Orr's Island.* Crown 8vo, 5s.*

———— *Little Pussey Willow.* Fcap., 2s.

* *See also* Rose Library.

Stowe (Mrs. Beecher) Woman in Sacred History. Illustrated with 15 Chromo-lithographs and about 200 pages of Letterpress. Demy 4to, cloth extra, gilt edges, 25*s.*

Student's French Examiner. By F. JULIEN, Author of " Petites Leçons de Conversation et de Grammaire." Square crown 8vo, cloth, 2*s.*

Studies in German Literature. By BAYARD TAYLOR. Edited by MARIE TAYLOR. With an Introduction by the Hon. GEORGE H. BOKER. 8vo, cloth extra, 10*s.* 6*d.*

Studies in the Theory of Descent. By Dr. AUG. WEISMANN, Professor in the University of Freiburg. Translated and edited by RAPHAEL MELDOLA, F.C.S., Secretary of the Entomological Society of London. Part I.—"On the Seasonal Dimorphism of Butterflies," containing Original Communications by Mr. W. H. EDWARDS, of Coalburgh. With two Coloured Plates. Price of Part. I. (to Subscribers for the whole work only) 8*s*; Part. II. (6 coloured plates), 16*s.* ; Part III., 6*s.*

Sugar Beet (The). Including a History of the Beet Sugar Industry in Europe, Varieties of the Sugar Beet, Examination, Soils, Tillage, Seeds and Sowing, Yield and Cost of Cultivation, Harvesting, Transportation, Conservation, Feeding Qualities of the Beet and of the Pulp, &c. By L. S. WARE. Illustrated. 8vo, cloth extra, 21*s.*

Sullivan (A. M., M.P.). See " New Ireland."

Sulphuric Acid (A Practical Treatise on the Manufacture of). By A. G. and C. G. LOCK, Consulting Chemical Engineers. With 77 Construction Plates, and other Illustrations.

Sumner (Hon. Charles). See Life and Letters.

Sunrise: A Story of These Times. By WILLIAM BLACK, Author of " A Daughter of Heth," &c. To be published in 15 Monthly Parts, commencing April 1st, 1*s.* each.

Surgeon's Handbook on the Treatment of Wounded in War. By Dr. FRIEDRICH ESMARCH, Professor of Surgery in the University of Kiel, and Surgeon-General to the Prussian Army. Translated by H. H. CLUTTON, B.A. Cantab, F.R.C.S. Numerous Coloured Plates and Illustrations, 8vo, strongly bound in flexible leather, 1*l.* 8*s.*

Sylvan Spring. By FRANCIS GEORGE HEATH. Illustrated by 12 Coloured Plates, drawn by F. E. HULME, F.L.S., Artist and Author of " Familiar Wild Flowers;" by 16 full-page, and more than 100 other Wood Engravings. Large post 8vo, cloth, gilt edges, 12*s.* 6*d.*

TAUCHNITZ'S English Editions of German Authors.
Each volume, cloth flexible, 2s. ; or sewed, 1s. 6d. (Catalogues post free on application.)

—————— (B.) *German and English Dictionary.* Cloth, 1s. 6d.; roan, 2s.

—————— *French and English.* Paper, 1s. 6d.; cloth, 2s.; roan, 2s. 6d.

—————— *Italian and English.* Paper, 1s. 6d.; cloth, 2s.; roan, 2s. 6d.

—————— *Spanish and English.* Paper, 1s. 6d.; cloth, 2s.; roan, 2s. 6d.

—————— *New Testament.* Cloth, 2s.; gilt, 2s. 6d.

Taylor (Bayard). See " Studies in German Literature."

Textbook (A) of Harmony. For the Use of Schools and Students. By the late CHARLES EDWARD HORSLEY. Revised for the Press by WESTLEY RICHARDS and W. H. CALCOTT. Small post 8vo, cloth extra, 3s. 6d.

Through the Dark Continent : The Sources of the Nile ; Around the Great Lakes, and down the Congo. By HENRY M. STANLEY. 2 vols., demy 8vo, containing 150 Full-page and other Illustrations, 2 Portraits of the Author, and 10 Maps, 42s. Seventh Thousand. Cheaper Edition, crown 8vo, with some of the Illustrations and Maps. 1 vol., 12s. 6d.

Tour of the Prince of Wales in India. See RUSSELL.

Trees and Ferns. By F. G. HEATH. Crown 8vo, cloth, gilt edges, with numerous Illustrations, 3s. 6d.
"A charming little volume."—*Land and Water.*

Turkistan. Notes of a Journey in the Russian Provinces of Central Asia and the Khanates of Bokhara and Kokand. By EUGENE SCHUYLER, Late Secretary to the American Legation, St. Petersburg. Numerous Illustrations. 2 vols, 8vo, cloth extra, 5th Edition, 2l. 2s.

Two Friends. By LUCIEN BIART, Author of " Adventures of a Young Naturalist," " My Rambles in the New World," &c. Small post 8vo, numerous Illustrations, gilt edges, 7s. 6d. ; plainer binding, 5s.

Two Supercargoes (The) ; or, Adventures in Savage Africa. By W. H. G. KINGSTON. Numerous Full-page Illustrations. Square imperial 16mo, cloth extra, gilt edges, 7s. 6d. ; plainer binding, 5s.

UP and Down ; or, Fifty Years' Experiences in Australia, California, New Zealand, India, China, and the South Pacific. Being the Life History of Capt. W. J. BARRY. Written by Himself. With several Illustrations. Crown 8vo, cloth extra, 8s. 6d.

"*Jules Verne, that Prince of Story-tellers.*"—Times.

BOOKS BY JULES VERNE.

LARGE CROWN 8vo . . .	Containing 350 to 600 pp. and from 50 to 100 full-page illustrations.		Containing the whole of the text with some illustrations.	
WORKS.	In very handsome cloth binding, gilt edges.	In plainer binding, plain edges.	In cloth binding, gilt edges, smaller type.	Coloured Boards.
	s. d.	*s. d.*	*s. d.*	
Twenty Thousand Leagues under the Sea. Part I. Ditto. Part II.	10 6	5 0	3 6	2 vols., 1s. each.
Hector Servadac . . .	10 6	5 0		
The Fur Country . . .	10 6	5 0	3 6	2 vols., 1s. each.
From the Earth to the Moon and a Trip round it	10 6	5 0	2 vols., 2s. each.	2 vols., 1s. each.
Michael Strogoff, the Courier of the Czar . .	10 6	5 0		
Dick Sands, the Boy Captain	10 6			*s. d.*
Five Weeks in a Balloon .	7 6	3 6	2 0	1 0
Adventures of Three Englishmen and Three Russians	7 6	3 6	2 0	1 0
Around the World in Eighty Days	7 6	3 6	2 0	1 0
A Floating City				1 0
The Blockade Runners .	7 6	3 6	2 0	1 0
Dr. Ox's Experiment . .			2 0	1 0
Master Zacharius . . .			2 0	1 0
A Drama in the Air . .	7 6	3 6	2 0	1 0
A Winter amid the Ice .			2 0	1 0
The Survivors of the "Chancellor". . . .	7 6	3 6	2 0	2 vols. 1s. each.
Martin Paz			2 0	1 0
THE MYSTERIOUS ISLAND, 3 vols. :—	22 6	10 6	6 0	3 0
Vol. I. Dropped from the Clouds	7 6	3 6	2 0	1 0
Vol. II. Abandoned . .	7 6	3 6	2 0	1 0
Vol. III. Secret of the Island	7 6	3 6	2 0	1 0
The Child of the Cavern .	7 6	3 6		
The Begum's Fortune . .	7 6			
The Tribulations of a Chinaman	7 6			

CELEBRATED TRAVELS AND TRAVELLERS. 3 vols. Demy 8vo, 600 pp., upwards of 100 full-page illustrations, 12s. 6d.; gilt edges, 14s. each :—
(1) THE EXPLORATION OF THE WORLD.
(2) THE GREAT NAVIGATORS OF THE EIGHTEENTH CENTURY.
(3) THE EXPLORERS OF THE NINETEENTH CENTURY. (*In the Press.*)

492066

WALLER (Rev. C. H.) The Names on the Gates of Pearl, and other Studies. By the Rev. C. H. WALLER, M.A. Second edition. Crown 8vo, cloth extra, 6s.

—— *A Grammar and Analytical Vocabulary of the Words in* the Greek Testament. Compiled from Brüder's Concordance. For the use of Divinity Students and Greek Testament Classes. By the Rev. C. H. WALLER, M.A. Part I., The Grammar. Small post 8vo, cloth, 2s. 6d. Part II. The Vocabulary, 2s. 6d.

—— *Adoption and the Covenant.* Some Thoughts on Confirmation. Super-royal 16mo, cloth limp, 2s. 6d.

Wanderings in the Western Land. By A. PENDARVES VIVIAN, M.P. With many Illustrations from Drawings by Mr. BIERSTADT and the Author, and 3 Maps. 1 vol., demy 8vo, cloth extra, 18s.

War in Bulgaria: a Narrative of Personal Experiences. By LIEUTENANT-GENERAL VALENTINE BAKER PASHA. Maps and Plans of Battles. 2 vols., demy 8vo, cloth extra, 2l. 2s.

Warner (C. D.) My Summer in a Garden. Rose Library, 1s.

—— *Back-log Studies.* Boards, 1s. 6d.; cloth, 2s.

—— *In the Wilderness.* Rose Library, 1s.

—— *Mummies and Moslems.* 8vo, cloth, 12s.

Weaving. See " History and Principles."

Whitney (Mrs. A. D. T.) Hitherto. Small post 8vo, 3s. 6d. and 2s. 6d.

—— *Sights and Insights.* 3 vols., crown 8vo, 31s. 6d.

—— *Summer in Leslie Goldthwaite's Life.* Cloth, 3s. 6d.

Wills, A Few Hints on Proving, without Professional Assistance. By a PROBATE COURT OFFICIAL. 5th Edition, revised with Forms of Wills, Residuary Accounts, &c. Fcap. 8vo, cloth limp, 1s.

With Axe and Rifle on the Western Prairies. By W. H. G. KINGSTON. With numerous Illustrations, square crown 8vo, cloth extra, gilt edges, 7s. 6d.; plainer binding, 5s.

Witty and Humorous Side of the English Poets (The). With a variety of Specimens arranged in Periods. By ARTHUR H. ELLIOTT. 1 vol., crown 8vo, cloth, 10s. 6d.

Woolsey (C. D., LL.D.) Introduction to the Study of International Law; designed as an Aid in Teaching and in Historical Studies. 5th Edition, demy 8vo, 18s.

Words of Wellington: Maxims and Opinions, Sentences and Reflections of the Great Duke, gathered from his Despatches, Letters, and Speeches (Bayard Series). 2s. 6d.

Wreck of the Grosvenor. By W. CLARK RUSSELL. 6s. Third and Cheaper Edition.

London:

SAMPSON LOW, MARSTON, SEARLE, & RIVINGTON,
CROWN BUILDINGS 188, FLEET STREET.

www.ingramcontent.com/pod-product-compliance
Lightning Source LLC
Chambersburg PA
CBHW020344030726
47496CB00007B/1990

* 9 7 8 3 7 4 4 7 2 1 2 4 0 *